Thinking About Becoming a Real Estate Developer?

by

Ted Ihde

DORRANCE
PUBLISHING CO
EST. 1920
PITTSBURGH, PENNSYLVANIA 15238

Dorrance Publishing Co
585 Alpha Drive
Pittsburgh, PA 15238
Visit our website at www.dorrancebookstore.com

ISBN: 979-8-88812-299-0
eISBN: 979-8-88812-799-5

Real estate development is about constructing commercial, residential, and industrial properties for investment purposes. In order to do so, a real estate developer should have a good understanding of fundamental real estate principles and a good understanding of how real estate transactions take place. To gain such an understanding, individuals looking to enter the world of real estate development might want to first obtain their real estate license.

State real estate licensing courses and the process of becoming a licensed Realtor could be completed within a few months. Whereas obtaining a college degree with coursework taken - and an applied focus placed upon construction, management and finance courses - might be cost-prohibitive for the individual who aspires to become a real estate developer. And very time-consuming as well. Yet, obtaining a college degree with applicable studies completed is often considered to be an ideal path to take when pursuing a career in real estate development. The most famous real estate developer today would be Donald Trump. Donald Trump obtained his college degree from Wharton, majoring in economics.

A real estate developer will want to attain an in-depth understanding of a number of topics which relate to real estate development. Among them? Construction, finance, working with contractors and subcontractors, and city planning. Thinking each of these topics through, let's look at real estate development and a land bank.

A real estate development project such as acquiring land bank properties is one potential market strategy a real estate developer can use. In terms of real estate development and a land bank, developers could begin their pursuit by learning about good processes that can be used to acquire land bank properties while at the same time, gaining insight into neighborhood revitalization goals.

Neighborhoods have stakeholders. Among these neighborhood stakeholders would be members of a city council. Many cities, such as Kansas City, MO, have active neighborhood groups. Neighborhood groups oftentimes quite accurately speak to local goals and objectives neighborhood members have. These localized neighborhood goals and objectives could be part of a conversation the developer could initiate while he or she is assessing the potential acquisition of land bank properties.

The Realtor. Whereas the skill sets and the license the Realtor has could be useful in relation to the acquisition of and the future sale of improved land bank properties, in this example, these skill sets could be effectively integrated with neighborhood stakeholder initiatives - a wise integration for the developer to think through prior to taking on a real estate development project which includes the acquisition of land bank properties.

Real estate development is not a one-person ordeal. So building a good development team is a recommended early step for an aspiring real estate developer to take. Securing financing for the development project is key. Securing the necessary financing to fund the proposed development project should be prioritized early on by an aspiring real estate developer. How would one accomplish this?

Obtaining qualified referrals to banks, starting with local banks, while also obtaining qualified referrals to good finance companies and to loan officers with a track record of providing financing for comparable real estate development projects is a good idea.

A real estate developer will want to add an experienced architect, engineer and lawyer to their development team. Putting together a wise marketing strategy for the proposed development project is a task that could be merged into responsibilities bestowed upon the developer's Realtor. A lawyer does not list and sell homes. A Realtor does not design home build plans. An architect does not arrange financing. An engineer does not review contracts. So using a team-approach in real estate development is recommended.

Identifying a Realtor with local market expertise is important. A reputable Realtor who possesses a strong neighborhood focus will be able to provide accurate market data to the developer and to prospective home buyers. This includes neighborhood property values, as well as the number of days - *i.e.:* days on market (D.O.M.) - it generally takes for comparable neighborhood homes listed on the MLS to sell at prices which mirror projected sale prices within the proposed development proposal.

"Comps." These would be recent sale prices of similar comparable homes. The developer's Realtor can get good comps through their local MLS. How long it is projected to take to sell a home which is comparable to the home the developer plans to build could enable the developer to gauge his or her anticipated carrying costs for their project. Carrying costs should not be overlooked by an aspiring developer.

Speaking to how a real estate developer will want to garner local expertise which reaches beyond the process of acquiring and selling a property, let's look at how a real estate developer could assess the landscape while approaching a real estate development project through a municipality by involving municipality stakeholders. This next section consists of potential wording and processes a real estate developer might consider when contemplating whether to embark upon a real estate development project which is centered upon acquiring city-owned properties...with an eye on integrating local neighborhood initiatives into their real estate development proposal.

Proposed Developer Introduction Letter (to be sent to to a municipality)

___________ prioritizes transitioning city-owned properties into productive use. While doing so in a way which creates jobs within local neighborhoods. As developers, we place an emphasis on transitioning city-owned properties to projects which speak to the provision of affordable housing.

Affordable housing goals can start with establishing processes to increase access to affordable home loans - home loans used by members of the neighborhood to finance the acquisition of an affordable home. Through our Development Proposal prospective home buyers in ___________ will have reliable access to affordable home loans. Oftentimes, these will be home loans which require a minimum down payment.

Sometimes, a state and/or a city will have in place good down payment assistance programs for qualified home buyers. Through down payment assistance programs, city or state funds could be allocated towards a home buyer's down payment. In this case, the real estate - *i.e:* real estate parcels within the proposed development project - could be coupled to the provision of affordable home loans. This speaks to what is oftentimes a municipality's objective - *a)* increasing access to affordable housing, and *b)* increasing access to affordable home loans. Our Proposal speaks to the acquisition of city-owned properties while also speaking to the provision of affordable home loans in ___________ , addressing each topic individually through Addendums.

A choice to make: Real estate development or individual property acquisitions?

Real estate practitioners who lack the necessary resources to become real estate developers could shift their focus towards acquiring individual properties that can be rehabbed, then later sold. These real estate transactions would be classified as "flips."

Flipping homes requires one to possess a less-expansive skill set when compared to taking on a full-scale real estate development project which is centered upon the acquisition of city-owned properties. Individual property rehabs do not require a full-scale development team to be in place, whereas an integrated development team is required in order to be able to take on a development project which includes the acquisition of city-owned properties. This is one reason for why there is a notably higher number of real estate "fix-and-flip" participants in the market than there are successful real estate developers.

New Home Construction Financing for Home Buyers

When buying your new home and opting for new home construction, financing the home build should garner careful consideration. There are options, and there are choices too.

When looking to finance new home construction it is not uncommon for the home builder to have a preferred lender, a mortgage company affiliation, or potentially a bank relationship might be in place. The home builder may choose to employ an on-site mortgage loan originator to assist prospective buyers of the builder's new construction homes. By providing prospective home buyers with access to the developer's on-site mortgage loan originator, a budget can be constructed for the prospective home buyer. This provides the prospective home buyer with an opportunity to have a conversation with an experienced mortgage professional in person, thus enabling the prospective buyer to ask the mortgage loan originator questions about the home loan application process and the financial obligation the prospective home buyer is about to take on. As well as whether the assumption of such a financial obligation at this time in the buyer's life is affordable.

In terms of real estate developers in the market today, Pulte Homes provides a great service to their prospective home buyers. Through Pulte, a home buyer has access to the company's online Mortgage Learning Center. Pulte's Mortgage Learning Center conveys useful information to prospective buyers of homes built by Pulte applicable to cost of living expenses, monthly mortgage payments and interest rates too. Learning about these can be very helpful, equipping buyers of Pulte homes with information they can use to make a well-informed decision, while in turn, also helping Pulte to sell great homes to satisfied customers.

A home builder may elect to utilize the services of an integrated mortgage lender in order to facilitate the retention of builder profits realized through sales of the builder's homes. An integrated mortgage lender could enable the home builder to offer incentives to prospective home buyers, potentially in the form of reduced sale prices, interest rate buy-downs and/or closing cost assistance.

When home buyers elect to secure their own financing to build a new home, the buyer might look into using a construction loan. In most cases, construction loans are extended to developers and home builders. Yet, construction loans are available to individual home buyers as well.

A mortgage loan is placed upon a structure that already exists. One example being: *When Buyer Bob submits a contract of sale with the help of his Realtor to purchase the home being sold by Susie Seller, Buyer Bob gets a mortgage to finance the acquisition of Susie's home.* In this example, Susie's home already exists.

Financing a home that will exist in the near future, a home that will be built, yet a home which does not exist today at the present time involves the use of a construction loan.

A construction loan starts off kind of like a line of credit. When opting for a construction loan, the buyer can finance his or her acquisition of the land they would like to purchase. He or she can finance the home being built on their land too...*i.e.:* the construction of their new home.

With a construction loan, interest is charged on draws which are used. When the home is built, the buyer obtains their permanent loan. A permanent loan is like the loan used in the prior example by Buyer Bob when he acquired Susie Seller's home. This would be a construction-to-perm loan. Two different loans. So, two loan closings.

The buyers of a new construction home may see a benefit by consolidating the acquisition of their land and the financing of their new home build into one loan closing, not two closings. In such a case, the home buyer may opt for a single-close construction-to-perm loan (SC CTP). The SC CTP is referred to as a one-time-close construction loan, or the OTC loan.

With the OTC loan home buyers start out with their construction loan. Their construction loan then later converts into their permanent loan. This conversion happens once the construction of the buyer's new home is complete. With this loan type - the OTC - the buyer qualifies only one time for both loans: *a)* their construction loan, *b)* their permanent loan. Each of the two qualifications takes place one time, the result of *one home loan underwriting process.*

In contrast to the OTC loan, the two-time-close construction loan could be a riskier loan to take on for home buyers. The elevated risk level incurred by the buyer with a two-time-close is attributed to the fact that a buyer's credit and/or a buyer's income could be negatively affected during the home build phase. With the two-time close construction loan, a reduction in the buyer's income and/or a lower credit score could adversely affect the *second* home loan underwriting process. Potentially prohibiting the buyer from obtaining a loan approval for their permanent "take-out" loan once the construction of their home is complete.

Another potential risk for the buyer using a construction loan to finance their new home build is: *What if the construction of my new home has not been completed?* In each aforementioned circumstance: *a)* adversely affected credit, *b)* a reduction in the buyer's income, *c)* a non-completed home build, *d)* a delayed completion of the new home build, the buyer qualifying for and obtaining his or her permanent loan - *i.e.:* their "take-out" loan - could be put at risk, and might not even take place. Whereas, with the OTC loan, home buyers go through their loan application process and their underwriting phase only one time. With the two-time-close, buyers might need to qualify two different times. The first buyer qualification would be for their construction loan. The second buyer qualification would be for their permanent loan. With the two-time-close, when the home build has been completed the lender may require the buyer to re-verify their income and their assets. Re-qualification by the home loan provider may be required so as to ensure that the financial situation of the buyer when the construction of their newly-built home is complete is comparable to, consistent with, and/or better than the financial situation of the buyer when they initially applied for their construction loan, which could have been several months or potentially even one year earlier.

Home loans: the 2 - 1 buydown

The 2-1 buydown is a real estate financing technique...an attractive home loan provision whereby funds are set aside in an escrow account at the closing *for the benefit of the buyer.* These escrowed buydown funds permit the home buyer to buy down the interest rate on their home loan, as the buyer's interest rate is bought down for the two-year period.

With the 2-1 buydown, in year one the home buyer's interest rate will be two percent below their thirty-year rate. In year two the home buyer's interest rate will be one percent below their thirty-year rate.

The 2-1 buydown is very simple. It is a two percent interest rate reduction for home buyers during the first year and it is a one percent interest rate reduction during the second year.

For home buyers, in years three through thirty, their home loan will have the same fixed interest rate (and the same fixed monthly payment). The buyer's interest rate (and the buyer's monthly payment) is set at the fixed rate the buyer locks in when they close on their home loan. That interest rate being, two percent above what the home buyer's interest rate will be in year one when using the 2-1 buydown, and one percent above what the home buyer's interest rate will be in year two when using the 2-1 buydown.

For home buyers, the 2-1 buydown has benefits. One such benefit being, the 2-1 buydown provides the home buyer with the opportunity to qualify for a home mortgage with a larger loan balance when they purchase their home at the outset. At the same time, the 2-1 buydown enables the home buyer to potentially purchase a larger home, or a home with more features.

In summary, a home buyer can purchase a larger home, a home buyer can purchase a more expensive home and/or a home buyer can purchase a home with more "bells and whistles" ...each benefit made possible for the home buyer through the wise use of the 2-1 buydown provision.

What does a 2-1 buydown cost?

The cost of the 2-1 buydown is equal to the difference between the principal and interest payments of the thirty-year note rate for the home loan and the principal and interest payments for the buydown rates established for the home buyer in year one and year two through the 2-1 buydown. The escrowed buydown funds are paid at closing by the seller and held in an escrow account for the buyer.

When are 2-1 buydowns used?

When a real estate market is softening. When more home sellers are putting their homes on the market - *i.e.*: increased inventory. When homes listed for sale are incurring price reductions. When homes are sitting on the market, unsold, for longer periods of time. Each market circumstance referred to above is potentially a good time for a home seller to consider implementing the 2-1 buydown strategy to sell their home (at their desired sale price) by providing this attractive 2-1 buydown option to buyers, thus in turn attracting more buyers to their home. Furthermore, when a real estate market shifts from a seller's market to a buyer's market, the 2-1 buydown could be a very smart benefit provided to prospective home buyers by sellers.

With the 2-1 buydown, the seller covers the buydown cost of the loan for the buyer. The seller provides this benefit to the buyer in exchange for the related benefit the seller can realize by selling their home at the (higher) desired sale price. This is done through the use of the 2-1 buydown by crediting the buyer with the buydown fees at the closing.

Interest rates increased substantially since the beginning of 2022. In an increasing-interest-rate-environment such as 2022 - 2023 home buyers face the prospect of purchasing a home using a mortgage which has a higher interest rate than they had recently been accustomed to seeing. With that higher interest rate will come higher monthly payments.

The 2-1 buydown can help to mitigate this "financial shock" for home buyers (attributed to the higher interest rates) while at the same time providing more home buyers with an opportunity to get into more home today at an interest rate (during the first two years of the loan) which is closer to the lower interest rates home buyers were seeing before interest rates started to rise.

It goes without saying that interest rates today are notably higher than they had been, early on in 2022. Families looking to buy a home today are taking notice of these higher interest rates. Higher interest rates affect family budgets, which in turn affects the terms of offers buyers choose to make on homes, which in turn also affects prices sellers are able to attain by selling their homes. Hence, sound reasoning for the use of the 2-1 buydown. The 2-1 buydown benefits buyers and the 2-1 buydown benefits sellers.

All said, using the 2-1 buydown provision in an increasing interest rate environment - *i.e.:* 2022 - 2023 - can position the home a seller is intent on selling as an attractive option in the market to more prospective home buyers when compared to comparable homes a buyer may consider purchasing which do not provide the attractive 2-1 buydown provision. Therefore, positioning the seller's home quite well while enabling the home to stand out in the market when compared to homes which do not offer the buyer an opportunity to get into more home now with a lower monthly mortgage payment (now, as well).

The traditional mortgage industry might be ill-equipped to finance the number of new homes the market actually requires

According to the U.S. Census Bureau sales of new single-family homes in December 2021 - *i.e.:* new home construction - reached an adjusted annual rate of 811,000 homes. Furthermore, according to the National Association of Realtors, in 2021, sales of existing homes totaled 6.12 million. So, sales of new residential homes in 2021 - *i.e.:* new home construction - made up a total of only 8.5% of the overall U.S. residential sales market, as per total sales of single-family homes - *new construction and resales.*

Arguably, that 8.5% total within the overall market is a percentage which, it can be implied, is simply not adequately aligned with today's demand for homes when taking into account the limited supply of available homes on the market. This challenge is accentuated by the continual ever-increasing demand for single-family homes in the United States, be they newly built homes - *i.e.:* new construction - or be they resales.

With 6.12 million home sales in 2021 - and with over 90% of those 6-million plus home sales consisting of sales of existing homes- *i.e.:* resales - it may be logical from a market-perspective for mortgage company executives to consider building their home loan origination businesses in a manner which services what the market actually needs. That would be *higher numbers of new single-family homes financed and built each year.*

In this case, in terms of mortgage lending, today, the market yields an opportunity for mortgage lenders to earn the majority of their mortgage revenue by financing sales of existing homes. *I.e.:* resales, not new home builds. Sales focuses are thus applied accordingly by mortgage lenders: *to finance resales.*

In terms of profit centers and potential market share for mortgage lenders, the market simply does not warrant focusing the energy, the personnel, nor the resources of mortgage lenders towards financing the construction of single-family homes. The financing of new construction single-family homes makes up less than 9% of the overall market, taking into account sales of new construction homes as compared to sales of existing homes - *i.e.:* resales. This, in a 6-million strong annual home sales market.

It goes without saying that the vast majority of home loans obtained today by home buyers - *i.e.:* borrowers - are going to home buyers who utilize the mortgages they obtain to finance purchases of existing homes. These home sales are classified as "resales." Resales being, existing homes sold by home sellers. Homes buyers decide to buy. These are existing homes in the market, listed by Realtors, sold to home buyers.

Let's look at the home loan finance market in relation to the majority of home buyers today, since the majority of home buyers use the home loans they obtain to purchase and to finance… *resales.*

In financing the purchase of a resale, once the home buyer - *i.e.*: the borrower - decides to purchase their home - *i.e.:* the resale - the borrower obtains a home loan to finance that purchase. The mortgage lender the borrower ultimately selects has a few options. The mortgage lender can either keep that home loan in their portfolio or the mortgage lender can sell that home loan off in the secondary market. For home loans that are held by the mortgage lender in their portfolio, the interest the borrower pays each month through their monthly mortgage payment yields an investment return for the home loan provider. This is one way mortgage lenders profit from home loans they originate. It's a huge business for mortgage lenders: financing the acquisition of resales by home buyers. Because resales - *and not new home builds* - make up the majority of the mortgage market.

Furthermore, in terms of financing the resale of a home, if, on the other hand, the mortgage lender decides to sell the home loan in the secondary market, the lender is then able to replenish funds through the sale of that home loan. A lender replenishing its funds - done so by selling off the home loan in the secondary market - enables the mortgage lender to free up additional capital that can then be deployed to the origination of additional home loans used by buyers to finance home purchases. These are home buyers who are, for the most part, buying existing homes that are now listed for sale in the market - *i.e.:* resales. Resales, which make up over 90% of the overall market in terms of sales of residential single-family homes.

Let's look at how the mortgage market functions…

In today's market, the majority of home mortgages are sold to investors through Fannie Mae, Freddie Mac or the FHA. The government sponsored enterprises - *i.e.:* Fannie Mae and Freddie Mac - can either package the home loans they originate as mortgage-backed securities or the government sponsored enterprises can hold home loans in their portfolios. Let's look at home loans retained by government sponsored enterprises - *i.e.:* GSE's.

When GSE's decide to hold home loans in their portfolios, GSE's earn revenue the traditional way - by collecting interest from borrowers when borrowers make their monthly mortgage payments.

A second profit center for GSE's, aside from holding home loans in their portfolios while retaining interest income received as borrowers make their monthly payments, exists in the secondary market. Through the GSE's utilization of the secondary market, Fannie Mae and Freddie Mac can purchase home loans, then bundle together the mortgages they purchase, selling off the bundled home loans as mortgage-backed securities - *i.e.:* MBS - in the secondary market. So the vast majority of home loans originated today go through the GSE's and the vast majority of home loans originated are being used to finance *resales.* There is substantive mortgage revenue available to mortgage lenders by financing *resales.* Resales - *i.e.:* sales of existing homes - consist of over 90% of the cumulative number of homes sold.

There is no question that a firmly established supply of mortgage money is available today in the market for home buyers to use to finance the purchase of their homes - these homes being, for the most part, *resales.* This ample supply of mortgage capital available to mortgage lenders is attributed to the hyper-efficient home loan origination model, the secondary market and to the GSE's. So there is a noted abundance - or arguably, an overabundance - of supply in terms of available mortgage money. Yet this ample supply of mortgage money is being used, for the most part, to finance homes which are selected by buyers from among a quite-limited supply of available homes. Whereas housing inventory is relatively low, supply in terms of available mortgage financing options, is very strong.

In terms of homes available to purchase, the supply of homes on the market has simply *not* adequately kept up with the supply of mortgage capital available in the market, relatively speaking; *More homes can be built. More home builds can be financed.*

According to the U.S. Census, over twelve million new American households were formed between January 2012 and June 2021. Yet during this same time frame, only seven million new single-family homes were built in the United States. So in terms of available homes to purchase, demand continues to outpace supply. Yet this demand could adequately be financed. Could be, that is, if there was an adequate supply of homes available to purchase. Arguably, home loan providers could substantially increase their profits if and when the supply of homes available on the market ever catches up with the demand for homes, coupled to the supply of mortgage money available to finance home purchases.

This being said, new home construction lending has tended to *not* be the primary focal point, *nor* the #1 focus, for what appears to be the majority of nonbank mortgage lenders. Construction lending which is used by home buyers to finance new home builds continues to be an area of expertise which is best-managed by local brick-and-mortar banks.

Financing new home construction *could be* a wise market segment for nonbank mortgage lenders to focus on. However, *Why build a home loan origination business model as a mortgage lender to service only a small fraction of the market?* This small fraction being, only about 10% of the market, as per sales of residential homes, comparing sales of new homes - *i.e.:* new home construction - to sales of existing homes - *i.e.:* resales.

Within the market, a segment of mortgage lending provided by traditional banks, primarily local community banks, continues to be the making of home loans the traditional way. This traditional way being, through the process of the bank first taking in deposits from bank clients, then second, making home loans to other clients of the bank. These home loans made by traditional banks are loans - as are loans made by nonbank mortgage lenders - that are used by buyers to purchase, in most cases, existing homes - *i.e.:* resales. This being said, loans made by traditional banks are also loans that can be used by borrowers to finance new construction homes. Local community banks continue to play a very important (preeminent) role in terms of financing new home builds. *Ie.:* new home construction. It's a market segment in which local community banks tend to do very well, while also being a market segment which is (arguably) not adequately focused on by nontraditional mortgage lenders.

The largest banks today are making fewer and fewer residential mortgage loans in general. And the largest banks are certainly making fewer and fewer home loans the traditional way. *I.e.:* through deposits. Furthermore, the largest banks are also holding fewer and fewer of the loans they originate in their portfolios. Fannie Mae and Freddie Mac own or guarantee just about 90% of all home loans originated in the United States. So the mortgage market is dominated by lenders who lend the non-traditional way, while resales - *not new home construction* - make up the majority of this home loan origination profit center for home loan providers.

While the nontraditional mortgage lender/mortgage banker loan origination channel continues to dominate the home loan market, the largest American banks are shying away from reliance upon obtaining bank revenue through this type of home loan origination channel altogether. The result being, the largest American banks continue to make fewer and fewer home loans each year as measured by market share of the overall home mortgage market. Yet traditional banks, large U.S. banks and local community banks are arguably the real solution that could step up, earn mortgage revenue, and fill a void in the market. That void being, a shortage of new homes available to home buyers. This is a void which is being exacerbated by, arguably, too few new home loans being originated and used to finance the building of new residential homes.

In 2020 nonbank mortgage lenders - nonbank mortgage lenders being home loan providers which are not structured as traditional banks - accounted for over 65% of all home loans originated in the United States. Furthermore, in 2021, nonbank mortgage lenders originated over 90% of VA loans used by veterans. In 2021, nonbank mortgage lenders originated just about 90% of all FHA loans. In 2021, nonbank mortgage lenders originated 70% of all GSE loans. Over the past ten years, nonbank mortgage lender share of Ginnie Mae issuance increased from 12% ten years ago to a staggering 87%.

So let's look at what the residential mortgage market looked like in 2020

Out of the top ten mortgage lenders in 2020, as measured by residential mortgage origination volume, only four out of the ten were traditional banks.

Looking at the top ten mortgage lenders in 2020, U.S. Bank came in at #10, with

180,649 mortgages originated in 2020. Bank of America came in at #9 with 184,118 mortgages originated in 2020, and Bank of America originated fewer home loans in 2020 than Bank of America originated in 2019. JPMorgan Chase ranked 6th in 2020, with 229,061 home loans originated. The top-ranking traditional bank, as measured by home loans originated in 2020, was Wells Fargo. Wells Fargo originated 320,026 home loans in 2020.

The #1 home loan provider in 2020, as measured by residential home loan originations, was not a traditional bank. The #1 mortgage lender in 2020 was indeed a nonbank mortgage lender. That mortgage lender? Quicken Loans.

In fact, Quicken Loans originated more home loans in 2020 than U.S. Bank, Bank of America, JPMorgan Chase and Wells Fargo combined. Quicken Loans originated 1.1 million home loans in 2020. Combined, Wells Fargo, Bank of America, U.S Bank and JP Morgan Chase originated 913,854 total residential mortgages in 2020. The residential mortgage market today is dominated by nonbank mortgage lenders. Yet traditional banks, arguably, have a comparative advantage over nonbank mortgage lenders when it comes to financing new home builds.

In 2021, we saw the continuation of a challenge in the housing market. This challenge? A limited supply of available homes for home buyers to purchase. This is especially true for first-time home buyers. Inventory is simply too low. Yet, while mortgage lending continues to be dominated by nonbank mortgage lenders who provide home loans to home buyers which are *used to finance, in most cases, resales*, an interesting, welcomed, positive footnote took hold. This footnote speaks to "supply" and is quietly emerging in the housing market.

In December 2021, privately-owned housing units authorized by building permits hit an adjusted annual rate of 1,873,000. This represented a 9.1% increase over November 2021 permit totals. The December 2021 total for building permits also represented a 6.5% increase over December 2020 totals. In terms of a trend, new home builds are on the rise. And more home loans as a percentage of the overall mortgage market will (and should) in turn be used by buyers to finance new home builds.

In January 2021, new privately-owned housing permit issuances totaled 1.7 million. In December of 2021, that aforementioned total was 1.8 million. New housing starts remained steady throughout 2021 - 2022 and the bullish forecast for new housing starts continues in 2023.

Whereas originating refinances as a home loan origination model for mortgage providers will likely continue to recede in a rising-rates environment, mortgage lenders will continue to pull back in terms of allocating resources towards business models which prioritize refinances. So, from a market perspective, local community banks, large U.S. banks, and nontraditional mortgage lenders, it can be argued, could be well-suited to consider shifting their focus towards financing new home builds. The financing of new home builds could be a good, fundamentally solid business model for nonbank mortgage lenders and for banks to prioritize.

Do American home buyers simply prefer large homes? Is it really just that simple?

Living space in a home today averages right at about 1,600 total square feet. The average size of a *new home* is about 2,500 square feet. The 2,500 square feet would be 56% more square feet than the total square feet of an existing home. Furthermore, the average square feet of new homes being built would have about 30% more living space than new homes being built in countries which have comparable economies to the United States. *But why is this so?*

OK, so in general, it can be said that European towns and cities tend to be more densely-populated than towns and cities in the United States. Yet, in the northeast corridor of the United States, this is somewhat not wholly accurate. The Northeast is just a fraction of the United States. *A small fraction.*

The Northeast has, generally speaking, a higher density population than most other parts of the United States. This we do know. So then we can use Boston or New York City as our examples, for the Northeast. Yet considering that most United States cities and towns are *not* located in the Northeast - examples being, Omaha, or Dallas, or Indianapolis, or Houston, or Phoenix - population density in the majority of American cities and towns would then not be comparable to population density in most European towns or cities, generally speaking.

Historically, the founding of our country goes all the way back to westward-minded settlers who fled Europe in the first place to settle in America. Lots of open space, coupled to unobstructed open land, linked to a sense of freedom. Further linked to the idea of owning one's own land and one's own home. It's just in our "American DNA." Always has been. Arguably moreso than it would be, in say, "European DNA," in relation to how countries were established? This simply taken from within the context of, *How was America set up in the first place?*

Westward expansion, the Louisiana Purchase, the Oregon Trail, Manifest Destiny, the Gateway Arch in St. Louis... Traveling from the east, which tends to be higher density, to the west, which tends to have far less density, is arguably, just, *American?* Examples being, leaving England for Boston, or moving from the Northeast to the Great Plains. It's just, shall we say, *American?*

The United States is composed of nearly 3.8 million square miles. Looking at Europe, the United Kingdom is composed of about 94,000 square miles. France is composed of about 248,000 square miles. Higher density *and crowded regions* is in many ways anathema to an American's historical perspective, traditionally, and historically. Higher density and crowded spaces, it can be argued, is just *not American?* The reasoning for this can be found in how sparsely constructed America is as a country in relation to say, Europe. Europe, that is, which is where this all started in the first place.

Looking at the Northeast...then let's think about Boston. Looking at the Midwest... then let's think about Kansas City.

Boston is composed of about 89 square miles...with nearly 700,000 Bostonians calling those 89 square miles "home." So now let's consider the far-more-sparsely populated Midwest. The Midwest, that is, contrasted with Boston. Boston, which is our Northeast city. And then let's look at Kansas City.

Kansas City, Missouri, added to Kansas City, Kansas (there are two Kansas Cities) is composed of just about 450 square miles. So Boston is about 20% as large - using square miles as our measure - as the two Kansas Cities added together - Kansas City, Missouri, and Kansas City, Kansas. Ok, so the two Kansas Cities added together consist of about 650,000 Kansas Citians.

This means that the two Kansas Cities added together have about 1,400 people per square mile. Whereas Boston has nearly 8,000 people per square mile. Boston is far more densely-populated than Kansas City. So building a smaller home in Kansas City - Kansas City being our Midwest example - does not necessarily make a whole lot of sense, relatively speaking, because either of the two Kansas Cities - *i.e.:* the Midwest - does not have the population density of say, the Northeast. Of Boston. Whereas building a smaller home in Boston could arguably make more sense because Boston just has more population density than Kansas City. Less room to build in Boston. OK, so Boston would be "Europe," whereas Kansas City would be "America," using our, *How is Europe set up and how is America set up?* analogy.

Another reason for why homes tend to get larger (and larger, and larger, and larger...) can be traced back to the United States government. And to the post-World War II era in the United States.

As the American economy boomed, post-War, the United States government essentially entered into the business of housing.

Post-War, U.S. housing policy backed (and still backs) the provision of home loans. The United States government is kind of in the business of underwriting home loans, in a way. When the government enters into any business, one can surmise that the business the government enters into - its size, its shape, its general construct, its entrants, its market behavior - changes. *Housing would be no different.*

The Servicemen's Readjustment Act of 1944, we more commonly know this to be the GI Bill, enabled World War II Veterans to transition from soldier to citizen. A gateway to the middle class for countless veterans was homeownership. Homeownership opportunities that were largely made possible through the no-down payment VA home loan.

Down payments, or a lack thereof, do very much affect what type of home, and what size home, one can purchase. Take away the down payment, then essentially one can buy a larger home - *the GI Bill.*

Then too, we should think about the United States Department of Housing and Urban Development - *i.e.:* HUD.

HUD was formed in 1965. HUD - see, low down payment FHA home loans. Low down payments? Then there is the increased possibility of purchasing a home. And a larger home too, by way of the smaller down payment.

The GI Bill, HUD, low down payment home loans, the government backing home loans...each functioning as a catalyst for housing and to expanded homeownership opportunities. The subject of the growth of the suburbs is then relevant too. In the suburbs one can build, one can buy and one can live in a larger home than one can build, buy, or live in in a city.

Then too, the United States government got into the highway business. Highways functioned as an additional factor for why homes tended to get larger (and larger, and larger, and larger…).

Highways in America connected homeowners in larger suburban homes to the offices they worked at in the more densely-populated cities. One can build a larger home in those suburbs than one can build in a city. Homeowners can drive in to their offices in the city from their larger homes in the suburbs. There's just more space in the suburbs to build larger homes. See the *Boston-Kansas City* or the *Europe-America* analogies as our examples. *I.e.:* open space, and a lack of population density.

The Federal Aid Highway Act of 1956 - the National Interstate and Defense Highways Act - led to the construction of highways throughout the United States. Those newly-constructed highways were then able to take Americans from their offices in densely-populated cities to the sparser suburbs. The suburbs, where there is just less population density. Paving the way - literally, and figuratively - for the building of new homes. Those were and are larger homes. Larger homes than homes that could be built (and were built) in the more densely-populated cities.

Ten years - 41,000 miles - $25 billion

Ten years and $25 billion represents what the Highway Act actually consisted of.

That is, $25 billion spent and 41,000 miles of highways added which could be used (and which were used) to take Americans from denser areas - *i.e:* from the cities - to less-dense areas - *i.e:* to the suburbs, where larger homes could be built. *The suburbs.*

Let's use Kansas City as an example once again

Interstate 435 in the Kansas City Metro Area traces its origin back to 1965. I-435 could take a Kansas Citian out of Kansas City, Missouri, - where a family may tend to live in a smaller home - to, say, Overland Park, Kansas. In Overland Park, Kansas, larger homes were built, can be built, and will continue to be built. There is just more space in Overland Park, Kansas, to build larger homes. More open space than there was in 1965 in Kansas City, Missouri. One can get to that open space rather easily - to Overland Park, that is - by taking I-435. So I-435 served as a catalyst in terms of why larger homes could be built and were built in Overland Park in the Kansas City Metro Area. It is today just as it was then: *the highway.*

Population density, highways, government policy and how America is set up as a country. Several reasons, interconnected reasons too, other than, *American home buyers just prefer larger homes,* for why homes in America tend to get larger (and larger, and larger, and larger, and larger…)

Request For Proposals: the RFP

A real estate Request For Proposals - *the RFP* - could be used by a township, by a city and/or by a municipality to couple bidders, in this case, service providers with whom a municipality may elect to contract with, and sellers. Sellers being the municipality.

The real estate RFP is essentially a procurement document. Meaning, it's pretty much a, *Here is what we need* doc. It's a procurement document in relation to processes or "tools" that a municipality has deemed to be value-adding for the municipality at the time of the RFP issuance. These are services which the municipality has at the time of the issuance of the RFP determined to be most effectively provided through outside vendors. Hence, the issuance of the real estate RFP. Hence, the opportunity for service providers.

Inclusive of a real estate RFP is a bidding process, followed by an evaluation of submitted proposals - *i.e.:* Responses. The real estate RFP is value-enhancing for a municipality in that the RFP helps the municipality to identify capable (and interested) service providers.

Specific to the issuance of a real estate RFP, a municipality could look to identify service providers to fulfill time-specific, service-specific and/or property-specific real estate objectives. Those objectives having been identified in the RFP by the municipality.

Within a real estate RFP, a municipality could provide a top-down overview for prospective service providers - *i.e.:* Respondents. This overview is likely to include details pertaining to pertinent information about, for example, properties included in the RFP. These could be properties that the municipality would be looking to sell - *i.e.:* to convey - at the time the RFP was issued.

Project-specific criteria that prospective service providers would be expected to meet during the proposal evaluation process would be outlined by a municipality within the RFP, as too may be goals the municipality is looking to accomplish through the RFP issuance. Then, through the municipality's service provider vetting process(es), each to be implemented by the municipality.

Competency demonstrated by responding service providers - *i.e.:* Respondents - will be assessed by the municipality. An org chart (organization chart), coupled to professional resumes for the prospective service provider's management team -

the org chart identifying key Respondent management team personnel - should be included in a Response.

A real estate RFP could cover many different topic areas for a municipality. Among these topic areas, the RFP could be issued to identify qualified commercial real estate brokers. Real estate agency listings could also be pursued by a municipality through an RFP. Property management services too. The RFP can include a wide range and an expansive array of real estate services.

If, say, a municipality has a goal to transition specific properties, or to serve as a catalyst in revitalization efforts within blighted neighborhoods, real estate development opportunities could be articulated within the RFP. If funding is sought, the RFP could include a request for real estate project funding proposals. A nice opportunity for banks and a nice opportunity for finance providers too.

Essentially, the RFP can be quite expansive in scope in that the RFP is able to cover a litany of real estate functions. Then the RFP will trend towards being rather specific in regard to its content once a Respondent gets into the "nuts and bolts" of understanding RFP requirements, as per preparation for the submission of a Response.

For Respondents, submitting a proposal in response to a real estate RFP could enter the Respondent into a highly competitive selection process. In relation to a real estate RFP, a prospective service provider could be seen as having comparative advantages by way of an ability demonstrated by the Respondent to effectively couple financing to equity. The Respondent's ability to do so would have been articulated for the municipality in the submitted Response.

In a Response, details pertaining to property acquisitions, debt allocation and equity infusions would be correlated to personnel on the Respondent's management team. Key personnel making up the Respondent's management team would have been provided to the municipality in the submitted Response, along with management team experience and proposed project responsibilities. Each having been articulated for the municipality in the Respondent's org chart. The org chart having been provided to the municipality as a supplement in the Response.

Sample: Introduction Letter sent to a municipality prior to the submission of a Developer Response

______ provides consultative services to cities adversely affected by distressed, vacant and non-performing properties. The ______ Client is a city possessing a disproportionately high number of city-owned and city-managed properties. Non-performing properties contribute to a reduction in property tax revenue for the city. The value proposition ______ delivers to city-clients is a Program the city can implement to identify, then to transition, distressed city-owned properties to qualified developers who proceed to rehabilitate the now non-performing properties, transitioning "bundles" of distressed properties to the status of "performing" properties.

______ approach to working with cities includes first researching towns and cities that are incurring ongoing challenges resulting from adverse effects attributed to the "big 4" - *1)* deindustrialization, *2)* suburbanization, *3)* "White flight," and *4)* the Financial Crisis. Cities with urban centers that have been disproportionately affected by these aforementioned macroeconomic circumstances constitute the core basis for the selection of ______ Clients.

The "big 4" - deindustrialization, suburbanization, "White flight," and the Financial Crisis - contributed to the hollowing out of city centers in American cities. Leading to decreased property values and to a reduction in property tax revenue. As well as to increases in city spending, spending allocated to managing non-performing properties and increases in policing efforts which are necessary to safeguard families living in neighborhoods which have become "crime magnets" due to elevated levels of distressed homes.

From an economics perspective, each of the "big 4" leads to increased city expenses and to decreased city revenue. There are additional challenges as well. Challenges which reach far beyond economics, such as neighborhood school closures, to name only one.

______ provides a consultative solution for a city which involves presenting proposed programs to the city, then implementing processes together with the city which could facilitate a successful adaptation to adversely affected center city environments resulting from the 'big 4."

Furthermore, the consulting services _______ offers to cities serves as a foundational "blueprint" for the city in terms of budgeting for increased levels of future property tax revenue the city can receive as a result of the higher assessment values of rehabilitated properties. Transitioning non-perperforming properties to "performing" properties creates "found" property tax revenue for the city. A focal point of the _______ value proposition to the city is based upon the "found" property tax revenue principle.

To take a general statement - *Performing properties generate property tax revenue whereas vacant, non-performing properties do not generate property tax revenue -* while transforming the general statement to a _______ solution for the city, _______ will develop a Property Tax Revenue Model. The _______ Property Tax Revenue Model has been designed to weigh the future receipt of property tax revenue against current city expenses which are stretched as a result of property tax revenue *not* collected from non-performing properties. _______ places an annual dollar amount on managing non-performing properties. This could include the mowing of lawns, additional policing efforts, serving owners, property maintenance and lost property tax revenue… then multiplying the cumulative annual loss per property, per year, by the number of years in the _______ projection.

Why _______ properties? _______ solutions-based approach favors transitioning "bundles" of non-performing city properties as the recommended revitalization process for the city to pursue, as opposed to sales of single non-performing properties.

Rehabilitating "bundles" of properties

The _______ Proposal qualifies a "bundle" of properties as a group of _______ non-performing properties. Ours is a suggested strategy which is preferable to a "onesies-twosies" approach to transitioning non-performing properties back to the market as "performing" properties.

One of _______ advantages is providing proven solutions to a city, whereas there are simply a limited number of effective market solutions a city can use to address challenges which relate to managing distressed, vacant, non-performing properties. Outside of a city-centric approach, the market operates in a "onesies-twosies" structure - *individual Realtors, individual home loans, individual real estate investors.* The "onesies-twosies" approach works well for the individual buyer, for the individual Realtor and for the individual investor. However the "onesies-twosies" approach is not an effective city solution.

Once the city's annual costs associated with managing ___________ non-performing properties has been determined, ________ will prepare a Proposal for the city contrasting the cost of managing ___________ non-performing properties weighed against projected annual property tax revenue the city could collect as a result of ___________ properties having been transitioned to "performing" status and added back onto the city's tax roll.

___________ will present the city with projected property tax assessment values for the ___________ rehabilitated properties by reviewing tax assessment values of comparable neighborhood properties which presently exist as "performing" city properties. "Performing" properties generate property tax revenue for the city. Non-performing properties do not.

Through the __________ Proposal, the city will have an opportunity to review our Cost-Benefit Summary. ________ will project a five-year, a ten-year and a fifteen-year Financial Analysis which is centered upon the net financial gain available to the city by transitioning ___________ properties back onto the city's tax roll.

By using the "bundled" properties approach in transitioning now non-performing properties to the status of "performing properties," the city's internal processes *and expenses* will be lessened. Furthermore the "onesies-twosies" approach involves handling more individual files, more paperwork and requires more personnel. *I.e.:* more city costs.

Net property tax revenue gains, *coupled to reduced city expenses*, coupled to an anticipated increase in neighborhood home buyer demand (and newfound buyer interest in neighborhoods being revitalized) will lead to additional benefits for the city.

Neighborhood home values of homes outside of the "bundle" of transitioned properties will increase, thus creating additional property tax revenue for the city through the increased tax assessment values of neighborhood homes. Each of these benefits will be articulated in the _________ Proposal for the city; each serving as a foundational reason to contract with _________ to implement the Program.

The _________ Program-approach with a city is required because "the market," left to its own behaviors - *i.e.:* Realtors, banks, real estate investors, "fix-and-flip" specialists - is simply ill-equipped to provide adequate resources in a manner which is commensurate with a city's challenges in any formative or substantive way when the goal is to reverse consequences brought on by swaths of distressed, non-performing and vacant city structures resulting from the "big 4." Each of the "big 4" having contributed to destabilized neighborhoods, to decreasing property values and to a reduced city property tax base. The market's inefficiencies in terms of an inability to provide any real "city solution" is the foundation on which our Program is based.

_________ will conduct process overview meetings with city stakeholders to gauge the following: *1)* processes currently in place within the city to address challenges attributed to distressed properties, *2)* ideas which can be integrated into existing city processes to improve property acquisition and transition processes. City personnel can potentially be used within the scope of our Proposal to implement the Program.

_________ will look for an existing city framework while analyzing potential starting points from which our Program can be enacted.

_________ consultative services will be offered to the city whereby _________ will provide an overview to the city pertaining to existing city property acquisition and disposition processes. The _________ overview will accompany our Proposal. The _________ Proposal will encompass a "global" approach to the city's challenge. For example, the _________ Proposal will establish a two-year goal to transition _________ properties back to "performing" status.

We will begin by identifying efficient and cost-effective processes available to city stakeholders that can effectuate the transitioning of the first "bundle" of non-performing properties to qualified developers through our Proposal.

One notable value-add __________ brings to the city includes the implementation of processes the city can use to establish ongoing relationships with qualified developers. Whereas the "onesies-twosies" approach to city property sales involves the need to attract large numbers of individual buyers and individual investors, by contrast, through the _________ Program, qualified developers will transition "bundles" of now non-performing properties to "performing" status. This will compound the positive impact of real estate development the city will benefit from through our Proposal.

The __________ Program will solicit, vet, review and qualify developers. Qualified developers can transition groups of distressed properties to the market as "performing" properties through developer acquisitions of "bundles" of non-performing properties. This is a more effective solution than sales of individual properties to individual buyers or individual investors.

Consultative services provided to the city by __________ will also include the use of future Requests For Proposals. In preparation for completion of a city RFP, ________ will research factors which affect the RFP approach. This includes a review by __________ of city-specific data such as: *1)* the city's Master Plan, *2)* city and state statutes which are applicable to non-performing properties and abandoned housing, *3)* statistics pertaining to the number of non-performing, vacant and abandoned properties within the city.

Consultative services provided to the city will include a _________ Report. The __________ Report will include a _________ Cost-Benefit Analysis. The _________ Cost-Benefit Analysis will draw a comparison between two potential processes available to a city which could be used to acquire and transition properties. The Cost-Benefit Analysis could be centered upon drawing a contrast between, for example, a city's potential use of, *a)* spot blight eminent domain and receivership, versus *b)* a land bank program.

The __________ Cost-Benefit Report will focus on pre-acquisition city costs in a receivership - spot blight eminent domain model, as compared to pre-acquisition costs in a land bank program. To arrive at detailed city costs for each model, __________ will obtain an organization chart consisting of city department personnel now involved in property conveyances.

The organization chart will provide __________ with an overview pertaining to available city personnel who could be used to implement the Program; potentially, current city personnel possess requisite skill sets and could be entered into consideration for deployment to carry out functions in a receivership - spot blight eminent domain model and/or a land bank program.

The __________ premise is based upon the opinion that existing city personnel will likely already be in place, thus acting as a hedge against needing to add additional city salaries as a result of what may need to be adjusted internally by the city through the implementation of the __________ Proposal.

Our position is that in determining the foundation for a Proposal, there could be a potential integration of applicable city and state statutes, taking into account city objectives which relate to managing non-performing properties. __________ will also take into consideration ideological preferences the city may have regarding the possible use of receivership or spot blight eminent domain as compared to a land bank program. The culmination of these factors will be reviewed and could influence the __________ Proposal. The evaluation of these factors lead to billable consulting hours for __________ .

__________ will develop a Qualified Developer Program for the city. Customization of our Qualified Developer Program equates to billable consulting hours for __________ .

The city will be contracting __________ to establish a developer evaluation process. The __________ developer evaluation process will be based upon assessing developer qualifications such as, *1)* projects completed (with pictures and sale data of properties), *2)* principal resumes, *3)* capital structure\financing, *4)* build specs, *5)* marketing strategies for repurposed properties, *6)* development team, *7)* developer narrative: *How this development advances city goals*, *8)* development completion timeline, and *9)* draw schedules.

There are two components to the developer-centered property transition phase in our proposed Program: *1)* identifying and vetting qualified developers, *2)* working with qualified developers to submit proposals.

Time allocated by _________ towards these two processes falls within the consultative category of ________ services, with payment to ___________ for _________ consultative services coming from the city in the form of billable _________ consulting hours. As developers are vetted and introduced to the Program, _________ will provide ___________ with projected cash flow channels, together with an ancillary opportunity to attract additional developers. Developers who can in turn submit proposals to the city either inside or outside of a RFP.

A two-city-meeting itinerary will be used by _________ . Up-front expenses incurred by ___________ include travel costs, a general expense account for business trips, meals, transportation and hotel accommodations (if the trip necessitates an overnight stay).

_______ will utilize a "Five Steps" approach in the first meeting with the city. The _________ "Five Steps" approach will be focused upon property acquisition and disposition processes. The _________ Proposal will be presented to the city at the second city meeting.

Areas of inclusion to consider in crafting our "Five Steps" for the first city meeting include, *1)* a discussion which is focused upon the possible establishment of a land bank, *2)* organizing a list of city decision-makers on whose support the establishment of a land bank would rely, *3)* obtaining a Status Report for non-performing city properties, *4)* identifying potential property acquisition processes available to the city, and *5)* identifying property conveyance procedures currently used by the city - *i.e.*: receivership, spot blight eminent domain, auctions, requests for proposal (RFP's)....

The first meeting with stakeholders will fall within the category of "non-billing." The first meeting is an evaluation. Time spent with city stakeholders during the first meeting will lead to no billing charge.

At the first city meeting, _____________ will evaluate the city's property acquisition and conveyance processes while determining whether the city has an interest in receiving a written _____________ Proposal. _____________ , by attending the first city meeting, assumes the need is already in place within the city. At the first meeting, _____________ focus will be centered upon whether the need the city has at the present time is paired to an interest the city has in moving ahead. Moving ahead with the _____________ Program includes the city receiving a written _____________ Consulting Services Agreement and a _____________ Proposal.

At the first city meeting _____________ will build rapport with stakeholders while establishing a date and a time for the second meeting. At the second meeting, the _____________ Proposal and the _____________ Consulting Services Agreement will be presented to the city for review. The second meeting will generally be scheduled within three weeks of the first meeting.

At the second city meeting - the _____________ Proposal Presentation Meeting - _____________ will conduct a full review of the city's practices which are currently in place pertaining to property conveyances. At the second meeting, _____________ will discuss the _____________ Proposal while making recommendations. The _____________ billing schedule will also be discussed.

_____________ will present a Retention Agreement to the city at the second meeting. The _____________ Retention Agreement includes proposed billable consulting hours. The standard _____________ Retention Fee is _____________ and is payable on the date the Retention Agreement is entered into. _____________ will provide the city with Monthly Reports as part of _____________ Consulting Services.

_____________ Monthly Reports will summarize steps taken by _____________ during the previous thirty-day billing cycle to advance Program objectives. Monthly Reports will include recommendations for the city to consider in relation to Program implementation. Program evaluation processes, progress, results, goals and timelines will be reviewed on an ongoing basis. Reports can be reviewed and discussed by way of video conferencing, a phone consultation or an in-person meeting with the city. We suggest monthly reviews.

Example: RFP Proposal Checklist

• Description of the organization's history, mission, staffing and organizational structure

• Articles of Incorporation OR Certificate of Formation

• Business Registration Certificate (if the organization is a partnership, a Bio for each Partner)

• Partner Bios which outline the responsibilities for each Partner

• Disclosure of conditions which may affect review - *i.e.*: bankruptcy, pending litigation

• Description of the developer's existing workload/description of recently completed property rehabs, complete with project descriptions, number of units, dollar cost for projects and locations/addresses

• Beginning and end dates of projects (with pictures of completed property rehabs/home builds)

• Proof of Funds Letter

• Accompanying ____________ Program Docs

• Proposed funding schedules/draw schedules

• General contractor resume

Example: Developer RFP Response

____________ has submitted a Response to ____________ and is interested in becoming an approved Developer through ____________ while working in collaboration with the city to acquire ____________ properties. ____________ understands that code violations will need to be satisfied prior to taking title to the ____________ properties, with a certificate of occupancy obtained for each property. ____________ acknowledges that ____________ does not require title insurance as a condition for property acquisitions.

____________ elects to order title insurance for each of the ____________ properties upon ____________ making the determination that ____________ is approved as a ____________ Developer, an approved Developer to whom the ____________ properties will be conveyed.

If ___________ provides notice that ___________ is unable to convey title to the properties, ___________ acknowledges that ___________ may elect to, *a)* extend Settlement Dates, *b)* permit the Developer to take title to the properties without abatement of Purchase Prices.

In the event that ___________ elects to enter into a Development Agreement with ___________, then subsequently terminates the Agreement, Developer acknowledges that ___________ will return the Deposit to the city upon the Developer signing a Cancellation Agreement. At thich time there is no further obligation and there is no liability for either party. ___________ will prepare deeds and any appurtenance easements at its own expense.

Developer will notify ___________ of proposed Settlement Dates by regular mail and by email. Proposed Settlement Dates will be no later than Settlement Deadlines. Developer notification to ___________ of Proposed Settlement Dates will be accompanied by a title report for the ___________ properties and will be delivered to ___________ by way of email and regular mail at least forty-five days prior to Proposed Settlement Dates.

___________ will notify ___________ as to ___________ acceptance of Proposed Settlement Dates. Should ___________ not agree with the Proposed Settlement Dates, ___________ at its discretion, shall provide ___________ with alternative dates for Settlement. These dates may extend beyond the initial Settlement Date.

At settlement, ___________ will pay ___________ - the Purchase Prices for the properties - with a certified check or by wire transfer. Transfer taxes will be paid by ___________. Real estate taxes, water, sewer, utility charges and stormwater fees will be adjusted at Settlement, pro-rata, on a daily basis.

___________ will pay the Performance Deposit no later than five days after the Delivery Date. Upon execution of an Agreement by ___________, ___________ will file the requisite applications, will pay the required fees and will submit required applications needed to obtain approvals and permits from ___________ while satisfying approval requirements within the RFP.

"Prohibition Against Encumbrances" - ___________ will not obtain financing for any property, nor place any liens, security interest, attachment, levy or adverse charge without prior written approval obtained from ___________. ___________ will secure financing for the ___________ properties. ___________ will notify ___________ no later than thirty days prior to closing on financing. ___________ will submit to a site plan, elevations and floor plans - collectively referred to as "Plans" - which are deemed to be instrumental in securing an approval. These will be attached as addendums . ___________ will enact development in accordance with the Proposal, to ___________ satisfaction.

Home builds will be completed prior to construction completion deadlines. ___________ will furnish plans which have been approved and stamped by ___________. ___________ will notify ___________ in writing if there are any proposed deviations in plans between the Development Plan and the submitted Proposal.

___________ will commence construction on the construction start date and will not begin any work on the premises until all required approvals have been obtained. ___________ has attended a pre-construction meeting with ___________ . ___________ has provided ___________ with a notice to proceed. ___________ will make no changes to the Plan - *i.e.:* no material changes - without prior written approval from ___________ and from city council. ___________ will provide ___________ with access to properties within twenty-four hours notice of requested access, as provided by ___________.

___________ is seeking to consider qualified developers to designate as additional approved developers for this RFP. Once developers are selected, ___________ will begin negotiations with developers, which will ideally result in developer designations by ___________ as Designated Developers.

Prior to the implementation of the ___________ Proposal, ___________ may have pursued processes to remove blighted properties before. We understand that vacant lots and non-performing properties create a hindrance to neighborhood revitalization. Vacant lots and non-performing properties adversely affect owners of adjacent properties. They detract from area property values, thus existing as barriers to the receipt of increased property tax revenue.

___________ will work together with ___________ to acquire ___________ properties for new home builds. Our new homes will be made available to home buyers whose incomes will not exceed ___________ . This creates affordable housing opportunities in ___________ .

___________ may exercise its rights through a Designated Developer. As such, ___________ is interested in becoming a Designated Developer in ___________ . Once in possession of ___________ properties as a Designated Developer, ___________ will maintain, safeguard and carry insurance on the ___________ properties while complying with post-RFP conditions established by ___________ . ___________ will secure the _________ properties; inspecting properties in preparation for new home construction.

Upon approval of the proposed ___________ home build Plan, ___________ will grant ___________ , as the Designated Developer, possession of the ___________ properties, *1)* pending the approval of the ___________ Proposal, *2)* subsequent to acknowledgement by ___________ that _________ is qualified to undertake the ___________ new home builds, *3)* upon confirmation that the ___________ new home build Plan represents a realistic and a timely way to transition ___________ properties back into productive use.

The ___________ Proposal includes a plan to purchase ___________ properties from ___________ , subject to ___________ and city council approval.

Upon receiving approval from ___________ of our proposed ___________ Marketing Plan to sell ___________ new home builds as affordable housing, ___________ will sell _________ newly-built homes on such terms - and at such prices - as ___________ authorizes. The maximum sale price for each of the ___________ new homes will be ___________ , with no home within the selected affordable housing pool of properties sold at a price to exceed ___________ . ___________ acknowledges that ___________ may elect to allocate a portion of sale proceeds to an escrow account, distributed to cover ___________ expenses/costs.

Proceeds from ___________ home sales will be distributed in the following order of priority: *1)* costs and expenses of sales, *2)* government liens, *3)* repayment of principal and interest on indebtedness incurred by the municipality and granted priority lien status, *4)* ___________ as the Development Fee; consistent with standards for development fees established for comparable development, *5)* valid liens and security interests, in accordance with their priority.

___________ will be the lead project coordinator in the proposed ___________ home build Plan. ___________ will be responsible for identifying ___________ properties and overseeing sales of ___________ of the newly-built homes as affordable housing.

___________ will outline project scope & development in ___________, submitting a Development Plan to ___________ for review. Once submitted, ___________ will negotiate Development Plan terms with ___________, amending the Development Plan if needed, as recommended.

Working with our construction partners at ___________ on the ___________ home build Plan for the ___________ new homes, ___________ will take a "surgical approach" rather than a "one-size-fits-all" approach to our development efforts. ___________ will ensure that our home builds are completed on time and will oversee the marketing of ___________ of the newly-built homes to new home buyers as affordable homes, while at the same time providing a new lifestyle opportunity for home buyers in ___________.

Sample: Developer Proposal

Organized in the State of ___________, ___________ is submitting our Proposal in anticipation of attaining designation as a Qualified Rehabilitation Entity (QRE). The ___________ articles of organization and Operating Agreement have been submitted to ___________ for review.

___________ Organization Purpose:
- To construct ___________ new single-family homes in ___________, affordably.
- To increase access to affordable housing in ___________ by offering ___________ of the ___________ newly-built homes to home buyers whose incomes do not exceed ___________ of HUD Median Income.
- Increasing access to affordable homes in ___________.

- Transition _____________ vacant lots in _____________ to affordable new construction homes.
- Revitalization of _____________ neighborhoods.
- The furnishing of staff, consultants, financial resources and related prior activities evidencing the experience necessary to carry out our proposed new home builds.
- Assembling a Development Team consisting of qualified professionals who will oversee the acquisition of _____________ properties and _____________ new home builds.
- Finance the acquisition of _____________ vacant lots.
- Complete the builds for _____________ new homes while transitioning _____________ homes to the market as affordable housing.
- Capacity is in place to purchase additional "bundles" of _____________ properties and to transition _____________ properties to the market as affordable homes.
- Home builds will achieve a high standard which positively affects _____________ neighborhoods.

The proposed _____________ Development Plan is based upon our acquisition of _____________ properties as well as on the implementation of proposed Development Plan details. _____________ is committing to act in accordance with established Development Plan schedules, as have been set forth.

_____________ will complete construction and will obtain certificates of occupancy for the _____________ properties upon completion of the home builds, while completing construction within _____________ days of Settlement Dates. _____________ will acquire _____________ properties subject to existing zoning classifications. Proposed zoning changes will be forwarded to _____________.

_____________ will carry general liability insurance in place with a coverage amount equal to _____________ per occurrence and with _____________ in the aggregate; conditions which will be established through the _____________ Agreement.

Improvements to properties will adhere to guidelines established through _____________ and will be completed at a minimum so as to obtain final certificates of occupancy while also meeting U.S. Department of Housing Quality Standards

(HQS). ______________ is committing to build ______________ new homes in accordance with HUD's Housing Quality Standards (HQS).

Property Sale Prices: the Developer Agreement

______________ will offer ______________ homes to buyers at sale prices which are not to exceed ______________. ______________ will work with ______________ on an ongoing basis to elicit pricing suggestions for ______________ homes, as well as guidance.

______________ will set aside ______________ of the ______________ new home builds as affordable housing and will establish an Acquisition Escrow account to cover appraisal costs, legal costs and pre-acquisition costs, as per ______________ suggestions. ______________ will keep a minimum balance of ______________ in the Acquisition Escrow at all times.

ACCESS TO THE PROPERTY: ______________ is seeking ______________ approval to physically inspect ______________ properties in our ______________ pre-build overview, agreeing that the planned new home builds will adhere to the ______________ Development Plan.

______________ proposes to furnish Quarterly Reports to ______________ while also providing updates to ______________ on home build activity and progress. ______________ will file a Notice of Completion with the court once each new home build has been completed (if necessary).

When no more than ______________ months remain prior to anticipated dates of completion, ______________ proposes to submit an affidavit to ______________ attesting that home builds will be completed within ______________.

______________ acquires and transfers real estate through mutually agreed-upon transfers. Types of transfers include traditional conveyance of real estate. Transactions take place between the property owner and another person/party interested in acquiring the property. Sale prices that properties are exchanged for are based upon how valuable properties are to each party and on the process by which property values have been determined.

Scope of required terms for property rights upon completion of the new home builds - __________ will market properties by focusing on increasing access to first-time home buyer programs. Points-of-contact for new home construction will be made available through ___________, home loan financing points-of-contact will be made available through ___________, and real estate contracts of sale drafted by ___________ will be available for review and will be presented to __________ by __________ .

___________has provided ___________ with __________ bank statements, evidencing ___________ in available funds (proof of funds). One certified check in an amount equal to the acquisition price (minus the deposit held by ___________) - will be made payable to _________ on the Settlement Date to cover acquisition costs for ___________ properties. ___________ in available Development Plan funds has been supplied to __________ to evidence sufficient capacity to complete the ___________ new home builds.

Phase I of the Development Plan consists of the first "bundle" of properties - ___________new home builds, with ___________in home build costs at ___________ per new home build. Phase I in the Development Plan will be funded through ___________ liquid capital.

Phase II of the Development Plan consists of the second "bundle" of properties - ___________ home builds, with ___________ in home build costs at ___________ per new home build. Phase II in the Development Plan will be funded through ___________ liquid capital.

Phase III of the Development Plan consists of the third "bundle" of properties - ___________ new home builds, with ___________ in home build costs at ___________ per new home build. Phase III in the Development Plan will be funded through ___________ liquid capital.

Phase IV of the Development Plan consists of the fourth "bundle" of properties - ___________ new home builds, with ___________ in home build costs at ___________ per new home build. Phase IV in the Development Plan will be funded through ___________ liquid capital.

__________ Development Plan acquisition and rehab capital outlays include __________ in property acquisition costs, __________ for Phase I home builds, __________ for Phase II home builds, __________ for Phase III home builds, __________ for Phase IV home builds and __________ for Phase V home builds.

Total Development Plan capital outlays - *i.e.:* acquisition plus construction costs – totals __________ , which will invested in the City of __________ through the __________ Development Plan.

Equity recapture involves selling newly-built homes as each Phase has been completed. __________ will make __________ homes within each Phase available to home buyers at prices of __________. __________ projects a sale price of __________ for each newly-built home.

Taking into account __________ in real estate commission, with __________ homes sold at prices of __________ , taking into account __________ in total real estate commission for the __________ homes, __________ in home build costs for the __________ new home builds, and __________ in acquisition costs, __________ projects __________ in Phase I equity recapture.

With __________ realized through sales of __________ newly-built homes in Phase II at sale prices of __________ per property, taking into account __________ in real estate commission, __________ in total real estate commissions, Phase II acquisition costs of __________ for __________ homes, __________ in Phase II home build costs at __________ per home build for __________ new homes, __________ projects __________ in Phase II equity recapture.

With __________ realized through sales of __________ newly-built homes in Phase III, taking into account __________ in real estate commission, __________ in total real estate commission, Phase III acquisition costs of __________ per property, __________ in Phase III home build costs at __________ per home build for __________ new home builds, __________ projects __________ in Phase III equity recapture.

With ___________ realized through sales of ___________ newly-built homes in Phase IV, taking into account ___________ in real estate commission, ___________ in total real estate commission with ___________ homes sold, Phase IV acquisition costs of ___________ , Phase IV home build costs of ___________ at ___________ per home build, ___________ projects ___________ in Phase IV equity recapture.

With ___________ realized through sales of ___________ newly-built homes in Phase V, taking into account ___________ in real estate commission, ___________ in total real estate commission, ___________ Phase V acquisition costs at ___________ per property, Phase V home build costs of ___________ per home build for ___________ new home builds, ___________ projects ___________ in Phase V equity recapture.

With projected equity recapture of ___________, ___________ will pay out ___________ of net project return to stakeholders while retaining ___________ in additional capital reserves which can be made available for subsequent ___________ development projects.

Cash flow to service the Development Plan is in place; ___________ has ample free cash flow to service the proposed Development Plan.

___________ has submitted proposed build plans which conform to recommended neighborhood design, home size, home style and architectural design preferences.

The ___________ Development Team will work with ___________ officials, zoning, city council, code enforcement, neighborhood leaders and design specialists to amend our build plan (if necessary) should our proposed build plans fall outside of objectives established through the City's Master Plan. ___________ will blend home build designs to conform to neighborhood goals, as per ___________ recommendations.

To provide ___________ with finished product examples for our proposed new home builds, ___________ has provided photos of completed comparable home builds. These are homes which are similar to our proposed home builds in *Build*

Plan "A," Build Plan "B" and *Build Plan "C."* Each Build Plan serves as a "snapshot" for what completed homes in __________ will look like.

So as to provide projected market data for transitioned properties in *Build Plan "A," Build Plan "B"* and *Build Plan "C,"* ___________ will supply __________ with MLS reports for comparable homes. Comparables provide market data for proposed home builds and can be useful for the projection of future property tax revenue.

__________ anticipates __________ will realize positive add-on benefits through increased levels of area refinances (and additional home purchases), each serving as a catalyst to neighborhood real estate activity; a byproduct of higher appraisal values and new bank comps. Area comparables are key to stimulating neighborhood home buying refinances. Comps thus serve as the home financing catalyst by encouraging banks to focus on the provision of home loans in __________. Higher home values and improved neighborhoods are ancillary byproducts of the __________ Development Plan.

__________ plans to highlight many thriving businesses in __________. Our goal is to build quality affordable homes in __________ while transitioning neighborhoods; increasing the attractiveness of __________ as a thriving community.

__________ will create a designated website for __________. Once approved, the __________ web site will be published.

Together with __________ community leaders, __________ will organize a "kickoff event" and will strive to get as many people to attend the event as we can. Our "kickoff" will be built around a thesis: *Improving neighborhoods one-home-at-a-time through the provision of quality affordable homes in* __________ . We have already selected a name for our event and we plan to further discuss our community involvement plans with __________ , once approved in __________ as a Designated Developer.

Police officers do an incredible job in the community. Many police officers would like to work towards bringing the community closer together. Community involvement programs will be encouraged. We believe these can work towards breaking down barriers between neighborhoods and the police. Establishing programs like these in ___________ will create a safer and a more trusting community. We would like to be involved in establishing these programs in ___________.

___________ intends to be a long term partner for ___________ . One of our company principals has already driven block-by-block to look at the ___________ properties first-hand. ___________ recognizes the opportunity we have in front of us to improve ___________. We will be here to make a difference. We want people to see our trucks, to track our progress and to get excited that improvement is coming to their neighborhoods.

___________ will have teams consisting of ___________ home crews while working together with city council to employ local subcontractors from within ___________. ___________ will be building ___________ homes at any given time. ___________ has the personnel in place to enact our proposed home build schedule. We have home design ideas which will attract buyers to neighborhoods without making our homes look out of place. This is a major point-of-emphasis for us as each new home we build will have its own personality. We have seen developers come into an area and proceed to make their home builds cheap - *i.e.:* "cookie cutter" - while not making a difference within the community. You will see a great plan of execution in the implementation of our Program.

As a Designated Developer, ___________ will build new homes which comply with HUD Housing Standards Quality (HSQ). Our new home builds (and our rehabbed properties) will increase access to quality homes in ___________ by transitioning now non-performing properties to standard housing which meets satisfactory criteria.

___________ homes will adhere to core aspects of quality housing, as per HSQ standards. ___________ homes will include sanitary facilities in each unit. Sanitary facilities will be in proper operating condition and will be adequate for personal cleanliness and the disposal of human waste. Sanitary facilities will be usable in privacy.

___________ newly-built homes will satisfy HSQ performance requirements both at commencement of assisted occupancy and throughout assisted tenancy or ownership. Home builds will meet acceptability criteria, as has been outlined by the Department, unless variations to our proposed development are approved. Anticipated possible variations could relate to local housing codes adopted by ___________.

Sample Developer Proposal: Building new homes in accordance with established HUD standards

___________ consents to the condition that criteria variations need to be in accordance with HUD requirements, pursuant to paragraph (a)(4)(ii) in Attachment F: U.S. Department of Housing and Urban Development's Housing Quality Standards (HSQ). ___________ acknowledges that HUD will not approve acceptability criteria variations if HUD believes that such variations are likely to adversely affect the health or safety of participant families, or severely restrict housing choice.

Acceptability criteria: *(i)* bathrooms will be located in a separate private room and will have a flush toilet in proper operating condition. *(ii)* dwellings will have a fixed basin in proper operating condition with a sink trap and hot and cold running water. *(iii)* properties will have a shower or a tub in proper operating condition with hot and cold running water. *(iv)* properties will utilize an approvable public or private disposal system (including locally approvable septic system).

Food preparation and refuse disposal: *(i)* properties will have suitable space and equipment to store and serve foods in a sanitary manner. *(ii)* properties will have adequate facilities and services for the sanitary disposal of food wastes and refuse, including facilities for temporary storage where necessary - *i.e:* garbage cans.

Properties will have ovens, stoves, ranges and refrigerators of appropriate size. Equipment will be in proper operating condition. Equipment will be supplied by the Developer or by the buyers, depending on conditions established within contracts of sale. Developer acknowledges that a microwave oven may be substituted for an oven, stove or range. Microwave ovens can be furnished instead of an oven and stove or range in subsidized and unsubsidized properties.

Properties will include a kitchen sink in proper operating condition with a sink trap and hot and cold running water. Sinks will drain into an approvable public or private system. Properties will have facilities and services for the storage, preparation and serving of food.

Space and security: Properties will have a living room, a kitchen area and a bathroom. Properties will have acceptable facilities and services for the sanitary disposal of food waste and refuse, including temporary storage facilities where necessary - *ie:* garbage cans. Properties will have at least one bedroom or living/sleeping room for each two persons. Children of the opposite sex, other than very young children, will have facilities provided through the redeveloped properties with each having their own bedroom. Developer acknowledges that children of the opposite sex may not prefer to occupy the same bedroom or the same living/sleeping room, as per HSQ standards.

Properties will include dwelling unit windows that are accessible from the outside, such as a basement or a first floor fire escape window. Windows will be lockable (such as window units with sash pins or sash locks and combination windows and latches). Windows that are nailed shut are acceptable only if the windows are not needed for ventilation, or as an alternative in the case of a fire.

Exterior doors, doors by which someone can enter or exit the property, will be lockable. Properties will be capable of maintaining a thermal environment which is healthy for the human body. Properties will have a safe system in proper operating condition for heating the dwelling units, and a safe cooling system. Systems will provide adequate heat and cooling, if applicable, either directly or indirectly for each room in order to assure a healthy living environment, appropriate to the climate. Properties will not contain unvented room heaters that burn gas or kerosene. Developer acknowledges that the use of heaters in the properties is acceptable, as per HSQ standards. Each room in redeveloped properties will have adequate natural or artificial illumination in order to permit normal indoor activities while supporting the health and safety of occupants. Properties will possess sufficient electrical sources so occupants can use essential electrical appliances. Electrical fixtures and wiring in redeveloped properties will ensure safety from fire. Living rooms and sleeping rooms in redeveloped properties will possess at least one window per living room and sleeping room.

Kitchen areas and bathrooms in redeveloped properties will have permanent ceilings and wall light fixtures, each in proper operating condition. Living rooms and bedrooms will have at least two electrical outlets in proper operating condition. Permanent overhead or wall-mounted light fixtures are understood to count as one of the required electrical outlets. Properties will be structurally sound and will not present threats to the health nor to the safety of occupants. Structures of properties will be in good condition. Ceilings, walls and floors will not have serious defects. In "serious defects" the Developer is acknowledging that ceilings, walls, and floors will not possess bulging or leaning, large holes, loose surface materials, severe buckling, missing parts nor other serious damage. Roofs restored or added to each property will be structurally sound and weathertight.

Exterior wall structures and surfaces will not have serious defects. In serious defects, the Developer is acknowledging that exterior walls and surfaces will not have any leaning, buckling, sagging, large holes or defects that may result in air infiltration or vermin infestation. The condition of interior and exterior stairs, halls, porches, walkways etc. will not present a danger of tripping or falling.

Developer acknowledges that broken steps, missing steps or loose boards are not acceptable, as per HSQ standards. Properties will be free of pollutants in the air at levels that threaten the health of occupants. Air quality within redeveloped properties will be free from dangerous levels of air pollution, carbon monoxide, sewer gas, fuel gas, dust and other harmful pollutants.

Properties will possess adequate air circulation. Bathroom areas in each property will have one openable window or other adequate exhaust ventilation. Rooms used for sleeping will have at least one window. Openable windows will be in proper working condition. Water supplied to occupants of redeveloped properties will be free from contamination. Dwelling units in each property will be adequately served by an approved public or private water supply that is sanitary and free from contamination, as per HSQ standards.

______________ will comply with conditions within the Lead-Based Paint Poisoning Prevention Act (42 U.S.C. 4821-4846), the Residential Lead-Based paint Hazard

Reduction Act of 1992 (42 U.S.C. 4851 - 4856) and will implement regulations at part 35, subparts A, B, M and R of this title, applicable to units assisted under this section of the applicable statutes and ___________ development standards.

Dwelling units in properties will be used and maintained without unauthorized use of other private parties. Properties will provide an alternate means of exit in the case of fire. Alternate means of exit include fire stairs or egress through windows.

___________ will build ___________ new homes, each of which will be reasonably free from disturbing noises and reverberations and other dangers to the health, safety and the general welfare of occupants. Neighborhoods and development sites selected by ___________ will not be subject to serious adverse environmental conditions nor to natural or manmade determinants such as dangerous walks or steps, instability, flooding, poor drainage, septic tank back-ups or sewage hazards, mudslides, abnormal air pollution, smoke or dust, excessive noise, vibration or vehicular traffic, excessive accumulations of trash, vermin or rodent infestation or fire hazards as per HSQ standards.

Except as outlined by ___________ , applicable to ___________ requirements and to HSQ standards, dwelling units will have at least one battery-operated or hard-wired smoke detector in proper working condition on each level, including basements (excluding crawl spaces and unfinished attics). Smoke detectors in the homes will be installed on each level in accordance with ___________ requirements and will meet or exceed all requirements set forth.

If a dwelling unit in a property is occupied by hearing-impaired persons, smoke detectors will have an alarm system designed for hearing-impaired persons. ___________ will get to work on Day One to ensure the following goals are met:

● Create quality affordable housing opportunities for residents in ___________ versus "just building homes."
● Build ___________ new homes, thus creating housing affordability while at the same time enabling ___________ residents to fulfill their dream of affordable homeownership…a dream many take for granted. We understand the significance attached to each and every home we build.
● Increase property values in ___________ . ___________ intends for current

____________ residents to benefit from our ancillary programs. If we can raise property values block-by-block, the partnership between ____________ and ____________ will be strong.

● Increase property tax revenue for ____________ . As property values increase, so too will property tax revenue.

● Clean up communities; not just building new homes. We see areas within the ____________ community where improvements are being made. We intend to be a long-term partner for ____________ .

● By helping to improve neighborhoods we hope to increase local commerce. This too will in turn lead to additional revenue for ____________ .

● Improve the perception of ____________ through our "wide net" approach. We understand it takes a *building-a-community* approach in order for cities to be revitalized. We have the building experience and the sales and marketing teams in place to make this happen in ____________ .

The following is a breakdown for ____________ three-year goal to transition ____________ properties back into productive use in ____________ :

● Obtain designation from ____________ as a Designated Developer.

● Obtain approval through ____________ to acquire ____________ properties through the ____________ RFP.

● ____________ of the new homes built will be made available to ____________ home buyers whose incomes do not exceed ____________ of the HUD Median Income.

● Acquire and transition ____________ additional properties back into productive use by building ____________ new homes. ____________ of the new homes built will be made available to ____________ home buyers whose incomes do not exceed ____________ of the HUD Median Income.

Our plan to attract buyers to ____________ includes employing the services of top real estate offices by enlisting their support and their enthusiasm for our Program.

We have a plan to celebrate each new home we build by inviting the community - along with hundreds of prospective new home buyers - to our first broker open house. Our broker open house will be held on the first Sunday after the first completed home has been listed for sale.

We plan on getting multiple buyers interested in each new home we build while at the same time creating a waiting list for new home builds. We will continue to come up with exclusive opportunities for ___________ and we are open to adjusting or to amending our Marketing Plan when necessary after each newly-constructed home is sold. Working with a reputable local lender such as ___________ will enable us to offer home buyers specialized services which relate to improving access to affordable home loans in _________ . Program benefits include:

- Low fixed interest rates
- Low closing costs
- First-time home buyer programs
- Home loans available to buyers with less-than-perfect credit
- Programs specifically crafted for ___________ residents
- Down payment assistance programs

We will sponsor monthly home buyer seminars to encourage ___________ residents to *stop renting and start owning*. Our seminars will take place at one of our newly-constructed homes. This way, prospective home buyers can see our final product while we walk them through the home buying process.

Social media advertising campaigns targeting renters in ___________ will be used. Our Team effectively utilizes social media demographic marketing. We can identify: *a)* current renters, *b)* individuals who just got a new job, *c)* couples who just got engaged, and *d)* those who just had a baby. Life events encourage real estate transactions. We know how to put our properties in front of interested parties.

We plan to hold seminars that will communicate to _________ residents the advantages of owning their own home, and how to responsibly manage money. Community events ranging from open houses, to block parties, to home buyer seminars, to events which benefit neighborhood children will be held.

Once ___________ has ___________ new homes built and available to buyers, we will conduct property tours for future home buyers. We can take prospective buyers to a few of our newly-built homes every month and invite them to a neighborhood breakfast.

___________ will install time lapse camera technology so home buyers can check on the progress of their under-construction home. After we sell the first ___________ homes, we plan on being able to add prospective home buyers to our waiting list. Buyers will be able to select their own finishes while knowing they are an integral part of the home build process.

Contributions to the ___________ Proposal will be made by ___________ . As a reference, ___________ developed a comparable Program in ___________ . ___________ has considerable experience applicable to real estate development proposals, property acquisitions, property rehabs and resales. In order to evaluate our Proposal, ___________ has provided ___________ with the following:

- Proposed build specs for the ___________ new homes.
- Pictures of comparably-built homes, evidencing home build design and style.
- A narrative speaking to how the ___________ new home builds will contribute to ___________ overall development objectives.
- Bank statements evidencing financial capacity.
- Construction cost estimates for the ___________ home builds.
- Personnel experience and qualifications.
- Development Team resumes.
- Summary of comparable projects completed.
- Corporate docs.

___________ understands there will be challenges. Our experience, transcended to ___________ through our Development Team, will enable ___________ to perform according to ___________ expectations.

___________ has the staff in place - coupled to dedicated resources - to be hands-on in ___________ on a daily basis. We will manage our home builds, together with our construction partners, by being present, on-site and involved.

We have provided ___________ with some perspective applicable to potential challenges builders and developers can encounter when embarking upon any

Development Plan:

1. Equipment is costly. It is important to keep our equipment in safe working condition. Our construction team has processes in place to do so - as well as storage facilities - and is able to transport construction equipment to work sites in ___________ each day.

2. Perceptions of the neighborhood: We know some neighborhoods we will focus on may have a less-than-optimal perception to outside home buyers. We intend to turn those perceptions around through community outreach efforts.

3. Educating the neighborhood about benefits which accompany neighborhood revitalization: Some residents may initially be resistant to change, wondering, *Why are these new builders here?* We will be open and transparent about our goals, communicating to neighborhood stakeholders how the goals we have established for their neighborhood will benefit not only their neighborhood, but the greater community as well.

4. Work hard to fit in while adding a superior housing product to the market. ______________ understands that some developers care about their product first and foremost. We care about our finished product too, and we also care about how our newly-built homes will blend in. We understand this can be a challenge. We will take a measured approach to each new home we build.

5. One of the challenges for prospective ___________ home buyers could be limited access to affordable home loans. To address this challenge, ___________ is working with ___________. Together, we will administer outreach programs in ___________. Our outreach programs will enable local residents to apply for low down payment FHA home loans (as well as down payment assistance programs, when applicable).

Outreach programs will be used in tandem with our educational *Home Ownership Video.* Our educational video provides a *"How to"* for prospective ___________ home buyers. Applying for and qualifying for a home loan will be made more realistic for neighborhood members. While credit scores could be a challenge for a portion of prospective home buyers, ___________ underwrites FHA home loans down to a ______________ FICO Score. ______________ also has broker channels available.

Where closing costs could present a challenge for some buyers, ______________ will work with our program lender while utilizing sellers' concessions, thus enabling ______________ to contribute to closing costs.

Needing a substantial down payment to buy a home - as well as money for closing costs - could limit prospective ______________ home buyers. By offering sellers' concessions, ______________ can reduce the out-of-pocket dollar amount buyers need to have available in order to purchase a home.

______________ will work with ______________ neighborhood groups and community organizations to introduce ______________ home loan products to neighborhood residents and will maintain a Home Buyer Pipeline Report. Our Home Buyer Pipeline Report will be emailed to ______________ and to city council members monthly. Home buyers who are pre-approved for a home loan through ______________ are recommended to be labeled "pre-approved." The loan amount each home buyer has been pre-approved for will be noted in our Home Buyer Pipeline Report.

Home Buyer Pipeline Reports will include clients' names, dates clients submitted their loan applications, home buyers' pre-approval status, the Realtor/Buyer's Agent, home buyers' down payments (percentage/dollar amount) and projected closing dates.

______________ will administer Home Ownership Education Classes which will provide an overview for the home buying process. By participating in our Home Buyer Education Classes, prospective home buyers will receive information pertinent to the home buying process while becoming "mortgage-ready." By completing our Homebuyer Education Class, prospective buyers will be able to schedule an appointment to meet with a ______________ loan officer who will outline the steps required to be taken in order to obtain a mortgage pre-approval:

- Submit required documents to the home loan provider
- Complete information required to be submitted to the home loan provider
- Obtain a free credit report

At the first meeting with ____________, questions will be answered about the home loan application process as prospective home buyers begin to prepare for homeownership. ____________ will review current debt obligations as well as other monthly payments to determine possible qualification for a home loan. ____________ will help buyers to determine a mortgage payment they can afford by reviewing the buyers' monthly income and expenses.

At this point, while not a condition required by ____________ , it's a good idea for buyers to establish a budget. A budget will help buyers identify opportunities to save money each month, while also enabling buyers to select a mortgage payment they can afford. A budget will also help buyers identify opportunities where they can reduce expenses. Reduced expenses create additional funds each month that can be used to pay their mortgage. Here are some factors ____________ will consider once a borrower submits their information to __________ :

- Required savings is maintained - *i.e.:* no "payment shock."
- Income is not reduced during the application and approval processes.
- Debts are not increased.
- Payments continue to be made on time.
- Additional underwriting requirements are adhered to.
- The buyer's credit report is reviewed in order to determine credit worthiness.
- Once a buyer selects a home and submits their offer, upon acceptance of their offer, the buyer's Realtor will submit the executed purchase and sale contract to ____________.
- Docs submitted to ____________ include thirty days pay stubs, two months bank statements and canceled rent checks. Canceled rent checks confirm that buyers have paid their rent on time over the past twelve months. For self-employed home buyers, twelve months bank statements will be required.

Typically, a credit score (FICO Score) of __________ is required by the home loan provider. ____________ underwrites FHA home loans for borrowers with sub-__________ FICO Scores.

For qualified home buyers with a manually-underwritten home loan which meets underwriting guidelines, a pre-approval can be issued. Furthermore, with supporting documents provided, and by articulating reasons for their lower FICO Score, it is possible in some cases for a borrower to be pre-approved for a home loan with a FICO Score down to ___________.

It is recommended that prospective home buyers meet with ___________ to discuss criteria reviewed by the underwriter which could enable the buyer to obtain a pre-approval with a FICO Score under ___________. Meeting with ___________ will enable buyers to determine what loan amounts they can be pre-approved for. This will be helpful when determining which homes to look at.

Once buyers have identified homes they like, time is of the essence to submit a full home loan application in order to close on the purchase of their home by the deadline agreed to in the buyer's purchase and sale contract. At this point, it is important for buyers to meet with ___________ to discuss what additional documents will be required in order to obtain their final loan approval.

___________ offers home loan applicants the ability to submit their information online prior to beginning the process of looking at homes. ___________ will review a borrower's debt obligations as well as other monthly payments to determine whether the buyer will qualify for a home loan. ___________ will help determine mortgage payments the buyer can afford by reviewing income and expenses.

Our proposed Development Plan will lead to increased employment opportunities in ___________ . ___________ is a leading mortgage lender in the State of ___________, with ___________ branch offices, ___________ employees and ___________ mortgage loan originators. ___________ closes, on average, ___________ residential mortgage loans per month. As a byproduct of our Development Plan, hiring local mortgage loan originators to originate home loans in ___________ will further increase access to affordable home loans, while also creating local employment opportunities.

___________ is interested in establishing a training program in ___________ to accomplish the aforementioned employment objectives. Areas of expected training for prospective new hires include, *a)* outlining a career as a licensed mortgage loan originator, *b)* establishing a state licensing program for qualified applicants, *c)* developing a New Hire Training Program for mortgage loan originators.

The _________ New Hire Training Program will enable newly-hired _________ employees to work under an experienced mortgage loan originator. Salaried positions as underwriters will also be created. There could be opportunities for local residents to obtain their designation as a Direct Endorsement (DE) underwriter. Training includes an introduction to Fannie Mae, Freddie Mac and FHA home loan products, the one-time-close (OTC) construction-to-perm Loan, down payment assistance programs and home loan underwriting.

A Neighborhood Program: Increased access to affordable home loans that can be used by owner-occupying home buyers to purchase and rehab neighborhood homes

_________ will focus on originating affordable home loans in _________ . These are home loans that can be used by owner-occupying home buyers to purchase and to rehab neighborhood homes. Increased access to _________ mortgage professionals will provide additional opportunities for prospective home buyers to qualify for affordable home loans.

_________ mortgage loan originators will provide an educational overview to neighborhood group members in monthly neighborhood group meetings while speaking about the following topics: *1)* responsibilities associated with homeownership, *2)* applying for and qualifying for a home loan, *3)* financing new home construction, and *4)* financing home renovations (refinances).

Applying for your home loan…

_________ will establish a system for in-person home loan applications to be submitted. This could be organized as, for example, a _________ mortgage professional being made available to neighborhood members on _________ between the hours of _________ and _________ at the _________ office and on _________ at neighborhood group meetings between the hours of _________ and _________ .

_________ will establish processes for neighborhood members which will enable online home loan applications to be submitted. This will lead to higher numbers of home loan pre-approvals being issued to neighborhood group members.

Steps to homeownership: Our "How-to" video

The _________ Homeownership Video can be used by neighborhood groups at monthly meetings. The _________ Homeownership Video is an educational tool which will enable neighborhood members to receive an overview pertaining to the following topics: *1)* transitioning from renter to homeowner, coupled to the responsibility of owning a home, *2)* applying for a home loan, *3)* different types of home loans available, such as FHA, VA and construction loans, *4)* qualifying for a home loan, *5)* working with general contractors and home rehabbers to determine what is involved in the construction of a new home or the renovation of an existing home, *6)* building a new home.

Home Rehabbers - Home Builders

The _________ Program includes vetting responsible home builders and home rehabbers to identify trusted teams of home build professionals who can then be relied upon to deliver quality home rehabbing and home building services to neighborhood home buyers.

Working with responsible home rehabbers and home builders to get construction professionals approved by ___________ as a means of making affordable homes available to buyers in _________ is part of our Program.

Neighborhood Homeownership Workshops

The _________ Program involves organizing Homeownership Workshops. Our Homeownership Workshops will be held monthly at neighborhood group meetings and will communicate to neighborhood members the availability of home loan financing options while also providing a reliable neighborhood resource for neighborhood members to plug into. This will enable prospective home buyers to further their education about homeownership while also providing them with the tools necessary to responsibly and affordably purchase a home, rehab a home or build a new home.

Program Real Estate Professionals

The _________ Program will add neighborhood-centric Realtors who are capable of providing trusted real estate services to _________ neighborhood members. Realtors selected for the Program will be well-informed regarding _________ neighborhoods. This includes having good working knowledge about neighborhood homes which are potentially available to be purchased and rehabbed in _________ . Program Realtors will also possess good first-hand knowledge of vacant lots in _________ ; vacant lots could be suitable for new home builds. Program Realtors will be well-versed in financing programs such as construction loans. Construction loans can be used by owner-occupying home buyers to finance their new home build.

Example: Developer Services Agreement

This Services Agreement (herein referred to as the Agreement) is made on _____________ (the Effective Date) by and between ____________ (herein referred to as the Developer) and ____________ (herein referred to as the Representative).

Whereas the Representative will endeavor to help municipalities sell or otherwise put their public and private abandoned, vacant and sometimes surplus properties back into productive use.

Whereas municipalities will frequently sell their own properties or encourage the sale and purchase of private properties within city limits through the issuance of some combination of a Request for Proposals (RFP) and/or a Request for Qualifications (RFQ).

Whereas Representative has considerable expertise in the field of non-performing, abandoned and vacant properties along with RFP-Q's and developer responses submitted in response to RFP-Q's. _________ has expansive experience relating to the sale of non-performing city-owned properties

.

Whereas _________ and/or _________ successors wish to assist _________ (the Rehabber) in the acquisition of municipal properties/city-owned properties to rehabilitate for a fee. Whereas ___________ (Rehabber) wishes to hire ___________ (Representative) for a fee to assist with the acquisition of ___________ properties.

NOW, THEREFORE, in consideration of the premises and the mutual promises and covenants contained herein, the parties agree as follows:

REPRESENTATIVE RESPONSIBILITIES. Representative shall solicit municipalities to endeavor to put abandoned and vacant properties within its borders back into productive use. Such solicitation shall be at the sole expense of Representative. The means and/or methodology of sales will typically be through the issuance of an RFP or an RFQ. Representative shall, as much as warranted, negotiate and assist the municipality in the production and/or the issuance of the RFP-Q at his own expense.

Representative shall then assist Rehabbers using Rehabbers' information by designing, drafting and submitting a Response to the RFP-Q (the Response). Representative's sole responsibility under this Agreement shall set forth in this section.

REHABBER'S RESPONSIBILITIES. Developer shall put forth their best efforts to submit in a timely manner the information needed in the ___________ Response, which may include use of the Rehabbers' logo and promotional material.

CONSIDERATION. ___________ shall be paid ___________ for each property that is conveyed to the Rehabber through an approved ___________ Proposal.

EXPENSES. Due diligence/property expenses such as title work, appraisal, survey and/or legal fees in any eminent domain or receivership case to secure title to the property shall be the Rehabbers' sole expenses. Expenses incurred by Representative in the preparation or submission of the Response, such as Representative's travel and payroll, shall be the Representative's sole expense. Any expense not specifically mentioned in this section shall be the Rehabber's expense.

TERM AND TERMINATION. The term of this Agreement shall commence on the date first set forth above and shall continue for a period of one year. Thereafter, this Agreement shall be automatically renewed on an annual basis unless one party gives written notice of termination to the other not less than thirty days prior to the termination of the term. Either party may terminate this Agreement at any time for cause. However, termination shall not relieve either party of the obligation to pay the other for work completed prior to the termination.

INDEMNITY. Each Party to this Agreement shall indemnify, defend and hold harmless the other party from all claims, suits, losses, liabilities, damages, judgments, awards, expenses and costs, including reasonable attorney fees, arising in any way from: *(i)* activities of such party outside the scope of this Agreement; *(ii)* breach by such party of any of the terms and conditions of this Agreement; *(iii)* failure on the part of such party to pay taxes, whether federal, state or local, or *(iv)* debts, liabilities, obligations of every kind and description owed by such party.

INDEPENDENT CONTRACTOR RELATIONSHIP. Representative is an Independent Contractor and is not an employee, servant or joint venture partner of Rehabber. Except as otherwise expressly provided for herein, no employee of Representative shall be entitled to benefits which employees of Rehabber are entitled to receive. Representative is responsible for all taxes with respect to amounts received under this Agreement.

CONFIDENTIALITY. During the term of this Agreement, and thereafter, unless required by law, neither party hereto will directly or indirectly disclose or use confidential information, records, trade secrets or any other secret or confidential matter relating to the Rehabber or Representative, or their clients, employees, business, products or services, whether or not it is labeled as confidential, without first obtaining the prior written consent of said party. This covenant includes, but is not limited to, disclosing or using information concerning customers, customer requirements, trade secrets, markets, costs, products, marketing, business plans or strategies, divulging the identity of clients or employees or soliciting clients or employees.

NON-EXCLUSIVITY. For the term of this Agreement and thereafter, Representative may do similar work for other Rehabbers.

NON-CIRCUMVENTION. During the Term of this Agreement, Rehabbers will not attempt to do this business by itself or with another Representative for the purpose of circumventing this Agreement, the result of which shall be to prevent the Representative from realizing or recognizing its fee.

MISCELLANEOUS. This Agreement represents the entire and final Agreement with respect to the subject matter hereof and supersedes all prior understandings or agreements between the parties on such matters. This Agreement may be amended only in writing, signed by both parties.

ASSIGNMENT. Either party may assign its interest in this Agreement to another qualified party with written permission from the other. Such permission shall not be unreasonably withheld.

SIGNATORIES. This Agreement shall be executed by ____________ (Representative) and by ____________ (Rehabber). Each party herein certifies that the signatory has the authority to bind the party. The Agreement shall be effective as of the Effective Date written above.

Developer Mission and Values Statement

MISSION

____________ is a leader in redevelopment projects which prioritize increased access to affordable homeownership for low-to-moderate-income families. Our development projects improve the quality of life for low-to-moderate-income families by revitalizing neighborhoods, without gentrification.

VISION

Stabilizing neighborhoods by increasing access to affordable homeownership, leading to the creation of employment opportunities within ____________ neighborhoods.

INNOVATION

The ____________ Program that we are able to deliver to ____________ is attributed to well-designed urban revitalization concepts. Our value proposition is an improvement over one-by-one, single-property, "big box," non-collaborative real estate development efforts. We take pride in our forward-thinking approach to neighborhood revitalization. Our Program leads to the formation of neighborhood "economic engines," leading to increased access to quality affordable homes and to the creation of neighborhood jobs, all while attracting additional investment to the neighborhood. The _________ Program is focused on providing quality new homes for low-to-moderate-income families while increasing access to affordable home loans in a collaborative effort with ___________ .

TECHNOLOGY

_________ utilizes cutting edge technology to deliver 21st Century benefits to ___________ neighborhoods. Among them, *a)* bringing to light expansive benefits realized through urban redevelopment, *b)* the promotion of responsible economic development within _________ neighborhoods, *c)* increased access to programs which advance financial literacy, *d)* the identification of, the cultivation of, and the implementation of good programs brought to market by forward-thinking progressive community leaders, and *e)* the establishment of programs which encourage entrepreneurship among women of color and minorities who live in predominantly low-to-moderate income neighborhoods in which _________ development projects take place. Furthermore, _________ provides ongoing training and job placement opportunities for ex-offenders. These opportunities can be coupled to re-entry programs.

SERVICES

_________ is committed to becoming a reliable ___________ stakeholder by bringing neighborhood revitalization Programs to ___________ through our unique ability to advance opportunities for aspiring real estate developers and co-developers who will come to learn about the value proposition found in our Program through ___________ city hall channels.

DEVELOPMENT

To facilitate a sustainable economic impact in ___________ neighborhoods by creating employment opportunities which will in turn attract additional private investment to _________ .

Developer Proposal: A Lender-Home Buyer Participation Program

Through the proposed __________ Home Buyer Participation Program, designated __________ stakeholders will focus efforts in a manner which addresses one of the key challenges facing prospective low-to-moderate income __________ owner-occupying home buyers. This challenge being, *limited access to affordable home loans.*

__________ will administer outreach campaigns and Homebuyer Education Classes in __________. Our classes will enable low-to-moderate income home buyers to apply for affordable home loans, thus facilitating purchases of __________ homes, leading to increased levels of affordable homeownership in __________ .

Increased levels of loan approvals for buyers in __________ neighborhoods through our Program will stimulate gains in affordable homeownership while attracting ancillary real estate development to __________ . This will create appraisal comps while leading to increased bank lending in __________ neighborhoods.

__________ will utilize __________ closing cost/down payment assistance programs as a hedge while cultivating good relationships with real estate developers who offer sellers' concessions to owner-occupying home buyers. This tandem of down payment and closing cost assistance, coupled to sellers' concessions offered by real estate developers will help to reduce the amount of money __________ home buyers will be required to have available to them in order to become homeowners.

__________ will administer First-Time Home Buyer Education classes in __________ while providing personnel to coach __________ first-time home buyers through the home buying process. Home buyers participating in the First-Time Home Education Buyer Classes will receive information pertinent to becoming a homeowner.

Your Journey from Renter to Homeowner

Buying a home is one of the biggest decisions you will ever make. Whether you are buying your first home or whether you are a seasoned home buyer you are bound to have questions. That's where ___________ comes in. ____________ will provide you with step-by-step personalized guidance in order to ensure that your home loan application and qualification processes and your home buying experience are understandable, simple, clear and timely.

Why stop renting?

A monthly mortgage payment is sometimes less than monthly rent. Plus, owning a home lets you build equity. Owning your own home means making your own rules without landlord restrictions. Meet with ____________ to learn more about the ___________ home loan qualification process. Determine how much home you can afford and get pre-approved. Be sure to find the right real estate agent and home builder. The right home builder, that is, if you are opting for new home construction.

How much of a home loan do I qualify for?

In order to determine how much home you can afford, ___________will consider the following:

Income
Debt obligations
Credit history
Cash available for your purchase

An FHA loan is a home mortgage insured by the Federal Housing Administration (FHA) and issued by a federally qualified mortgage lender. FHA home loans are designed for low-to-moderate income borrowers who are unable to come up with a large down payment. FHA loans typically allow borrowers with a credit score of at least ___________ to put 3.5% down on their home, thus obtaining a home loan which finances up to 96.5% of the purchase price of the home - or 96.5% of their home's appraisal value - whichever is lower. Otherwise, a 10% down payment is often required to purchase a home. The borrower's 3.5% down payment can come from a gift or a grant.

The Fannie Mae HomeReady mortgage and the Freddie Mac Home Possible home loan enable first-time home buyers to put down as little as 3% when purchasing their home. This is a lower down payment than borrowers would have by using an FHA home loan.

One prospective factor ____________ will consider when underwriting your home loan is possible "payment shock." Payment shock could be relevant to your home loan approval if your new principal interest taxes and insurance (PITI) payment significantly exceeds the amount you currently pay in rent. If this is determined to be the case, you may need to demonstrate that you are able to afford and to sustain your new mortgage payment. Remember, you will be increasing your monthly housing expenses by transitioning from renter to homeowner. In doing so you may not have excess cash-on-hand available for unanticipated home repairs.

If you do not take your increased monthly housing costs into account and study those increases closely, by incurring unanticipated housing expenses - such as home repairs - it is possible that you could run into financial difficulty as a homeowner. This is why it is important to determine how payment shock could be a factor to consider when determining whether you should purchase a home. Furthermore, demonstration of good rental payment history over the past twelve months, coupled to a pattern of "saving for a rainy day" over the same twelve months will enable you to attain a good understanding of the true cost of homeownership, which will not solely be your new PITI payment.

One other factor ____________ will take into account when reviewing your home loan application is whether there have been notable increases in your credit card balances from the time of application to your closing date. Increases in your savings account which correlate to matching increases in credit card balances could mean that you are using cash advances as a means to increase your savings. This would speak to affordability - or a lack thereof - and could be a factor ____________ uses to determine whether you will qualify for your home loan.

Over the past three-to-six-month period, your underwriter may look at the monthly difference between your new PITI payment, which could be higher, and your current rent payment, which would likely be lower, to determine whether you had been able to save this amount each month. This speaks to affordability and relates to what is called "payment shock savings." Your monthly bank account balances - checking and/or savings - should have grown each month in order to demonstrate payment shock savings. If you demonstrate one-time inconsistent deposits over the same three to six month period, these deposits will be sourced and the deposit amount(s) will net down the payment shock savings amount which is factored into the underwriting decision for your home loan. If inconsistent deposits are used to sustain an unaffordable lifestyle, paid for with the one-time deposits, this could be taken into account by the underwriter when determining the monthly PITI you will qualify for.

Two factors that will be considered when determining affordability are, *1)* your housing ratio, and *2)* your debt ratio. Each percentage will be considered by the underwriter so as to determine that you are not overextending. Overextending yourself financially could lead to a lack of affordability.

Your housing-to-income ratio is determined by dividing your gross monthly income by your new PITI payment. Industry-wide, an acceptable housing-to-income ratio is generally determined to be about 1/3. This means that 1/3 of your monthly gross income should go to your new PITI payment, with 2/3 of your monthly gross income remaining and available to cover other monthly expenses. A high housing ratio means that there may not be enough money left over each month after you make your housing payment to afford other household necessities or unanticipated home repairs.

Your housing ratio is determined by using your gross monthly income. This is pre-tax income. Your after-tax dollar take-home pay will be less. This means that while a "healthy" housing ratio is about 1/3 of your gross income, your after-tax housing ratio could be up to 40% or 50% of your monthly income, after taxes.

Your total debt ratio - *i.e.:* your back-end debt-to-income ratio (back-end DTI) - is determined by dividing your PITI payment plus your other household expenses by your monthly gross income.

Additional household expenses include gas, utilities, food, child care costs and other expenses that will continue to be incurred each month and which could increase once you purchase your home. Additional household and living expenses outside of your new PITI payment are generally considered to range from between 30% to 35% of your monthly gross income.

This means that if you qualify for your home loan at the maximum front-end debt-to-income ratio - your PITI payment as a percentage of your monthly gross income - less money will remain each month for ancillary debt service payments. These ancillary debt service payments might include car payments, student loan payments and/or credit cards. So qualifying for your home loan by not doing so at the maximum front-end debt-to-income ratio could be viewed to be a good idea. A 28% front-end debt-to-income ratio is generally considered to be an affordable DTI.

If you have been unable to demonstrate payment shock savings, the new PITI you are approved for could be based on a number which is closer to your current monthly rent payment. When analyzing affordability, payment shock, savings patterns and potential unanticipated housing expenses or housing repairs, a HUD-certified housing counselor can work with you to create a budget.

A budget can help you to determine where your money goes each month while also serving as a useful tool as you transition to becoming a homeowner. A budget will also help you to better manage your income and expenses. By having a budget you will see whether decreased monthly expenses leads to increased savings and whether increased monthly expenses lead to a reduction in savings. When each is realized, you can then determine a planned savings pattern while making adjustments for upcoming increases in costs attributed to owning a home. These are costs which include your new PITI payment as well as general expenses associated with homeownership.

Often, a new home buyer has a general idea as to what their monthly expenses will be only to later realize - after completing a budget - that their expenses are actually quite a bit higher.

Twenty percent of my income every month goes where again?

It is often said that 20% of monthly household income goes towards the unknown somewhere, somehow. Twenty percent of monthly income just kind of seems to disappear. By having a budget you will learn how much of your monthly income is really spent, yet not budgeted for. A budget will also help you to better understand where this money goes, while planning and adjusting for homeownership accordingly.

Oftentimes a family may be living beyond their means by using credit cards to cover necessary purchases as well as unexpected life events. It is possible, once you gain an understanding of your budget, that you may need to adjust your spending habits and your lifestyle as you get ready for homeownership. Then once your spending is adjusted you will be able to determine whether you are comfortable with the suggested reduction in spending which will be coupled to the elimination of some "perks" from your lifestyle.

If you decide to purchase a home that needs to be updated, FHA Section 203(K) insurance enables home buyers to finance the purchase of their home as well as updates to their home. These home improvement costs can be integrated into the buyer's mortgage. Section 203(K) functions as a unique and important home loan option for home buyers. When buying a house that needs repairs, home buyers can incur a costly process - out-of-pocket - thus in turn reducing available cash-on-hand, post-purchase.

Whereas obtaining home rehab money from a private lender could have a high interest rate, short repayment terms, and potentially a balloon payment which causes the home loan to be paid on demand, Section 203(K) is a viable solution. The 203(K) loan helps borrowers obtain a home loan with a fixed interest rate while providing funds for both the acquisition and the rehab of a home.

With a 203(K), a portion of loan proceeds is used to pay the seller. The remaining funds are placed in an escrow account and released as the rehab of the home is verified to have been completed.

The cost of the home rehab that can be completed through the use of the FHA 203(K) will be capped. The purchase price of the eligible property must fall within FHA limits for the area. The property value is determined to be the lesser of either, *(1)* the value of the property before the home rehab, plus the cost of the home rehab, or *(2)* 110% of the appraised value of the property after the rehab has been completed.

The extent of the home rehab which is able to be financed through the FHA 203(K) loan ranges from relatively minor repairs to reconstruction. Types of improvements home buyers often make by using the FHA 203(K) loan include:

- Structural alterations
- Home reconstruction
- Modernization
- Improvements to the home's function
- Elimination of health and safety hazards
- Appearance upgrades
- Replacing floors/floor treatments
- Home improvements that eliminate obsolescence
- Replacing plumbing
- Installing a well and/or a septic system
- New roof or gutters
- Landscaping
- Exterior site improvements

Do I need 20% down to buy a home? Not necessarily.

_____________ offers a variety of home loan options. Many borrowers do not need the traditional 20% down payment in order to be approved for a home loan. Down payment assistance may be available to borrowers who qualify. You may be able to buy a home with little to no down payment. Loans with less than 20% down may require private mortgage insurance (PMI).

What Is Private Mortgage Insurance?

Private mortgage insurance enables you to purchase a home with a lower down payment than that which otherwise may be required. If you are required to pay private mortgage insurance, you have the option to, *a)* pay your private mortgage insurance through the mortgage payment, or *b)* pay the issuer of private mortgage insurance as a lump sum at closing.

What are closing costs and lender fees?

These are costs associated with processing, approving and funding your home loan. Prepaid costs are typically collected in an escrow account to cover three months of taxes, insurance and interest.

What are 3rd party fees?

These are fees charged by 3rd party vendors in connection with your home loan. Third party fees include title fees, attorney fees and the appraisal.

How does my credit factor into my home loan?

A credit report shows the lender your history of past payments, illustrating for your lender how likely you will be to make your mortgage payments on time. Your credit score, which is also known as your FICO Score, can factor into the type of home loan you are eligible for. Your credit score could also affect your interest rate, your down payment and your loan amount.

What does a mortgage payment consist of?

Mortgage payments consist of PITI - principal, interest, taxes and insurance. An escrow account is established to collect money for your taxes and your insurance each month. The money that goes into the escrow account will be applied towards your taxes and your insurance as each comes due.

What is APR?

The APR - annual percentage rate - is a measurement which helps home buyers compare available home loan options. The APR includes the total cost of the home loan over the term of the loan. The APR differs from the base interest rate and is typically higher than the base interest rate. The APR includes loan interest along with other loan charges.

Pre-qualified vrs. Pre-approved

Pre-qualified: Pre-qualification is the initial step in the home loan application process. Usually a pre-qualification is issued before a full loan application is submitted. In order to obtain a pre-qualification the prospective borrower provides documents to their lender which illustrate the borrowing capacity of the borrower. Below is a summary of what a home loan provider will evaluate when determining whether to pre-qualify a buyer for their home loan.

Income
Assets
Debts
Credit score

Pre-approved: A pre-approval is a review of the borrower's financial circumstances by the home loan provider. The pre-approval is usually issued after a loan application has been submitted. In order to obtain a pre-approval, ____________ will review the following:

Credit report
Liquid assets/bank statements
Pay stubs/tax returns
Employment history

Conventional financing…also known as a conforming home loan

A conventional home loan adheres to guidelines established by Fannie Mae and Freddie Mac.

Down payments as low as 3%
First-time home buyer options
Availability of gifted down payments

The FHA home loan

The Federal Housing Administration (FHA) mortgage is sometimes referred to as a "government loan." An FHA home loan is backed by the Federal Housing Administration (FHA). The FHA provides mortgage insurance on loans made by FHA-approved lenders.

Down payments as low as 3.50%
Typically lower interest rates
Potential availability of lower credit score requirements

U.S. Department of Veterans Affairs (VA)

A VA loan is available to active duty service members and to retired veterans. The VA home loan comes with many benefits when compared with a conventional home loan or an FHA loan.

No down payment is required if entitlement is available.
Potential for lower closing costs.
Certain discounts are available for disabled veterans.

U.S. Department of Agriculture (USDA)

With the USDA Guarantee Rural Housing program, eligible properties must be located in a rural area as defined by the USDA. Applicants for a USDA home loan are required to meet established household income guidelines.

No down payment required.

A lower credit score may be accepted.

Cash reserves after closing may not be required.

The Jumbo Mortgage

A Jumbo loan is a mortgage with a loan amount that exceeds conforming loan limits.

Let's get started with the Program

To start, a prospective home buyer will complete their mortgage application. Buyers can start their application in a way which is most convenient for them. Either online, over the phone or in person. Here are your steps:

1. Get pre-qualified.
2. Decide on the home you would like to purchase or build.
3. Submit your paperwork to your home loan provider.
4. Schedule your home inspection.
5. Your home loan provider starts processing your loan.
6. Order the appraisal.
7. Your home loan provider underwrites your loan.
8. Financial approval is obtained by your home loan provider.
9. The final home inspection takes place.
10. The closing takes place.
11. Your loan is funded.
12. You are a homeowner.

Note: Down payment assistance may be available to first-time home buyers who qualify.

___________ will review your household income and your rental payment history to determine if you are in a position to transition from renter to homeowner. If you are able to transition to homeownership, you can work towards determining a monthly principal, interest, taxes and insurance (PITI) payment you can afford.

Obtaining your pre-approval will enable you to figure out how much house you can afford. Electing to work with a reputable Realtor who will guide you through the home buying process is a good next step.

While your Realtor will assist you with the purchase of your home, it is important to have ongoing dialogue with your mortgage professional throughout the home buying process so as to determine whether the financial obligation you will be taking on by purchasing your home will enable you to submit an offer to purchase the home. This will help you to determine affordability before you submit your offer for the home.

The condition of the home you are hoping to buy is significant. Homes with deferred maintenance - or homes which require repairs to be completed imminently upon purchase - can cause unanticipated financial obligations for the buyer. A reputable home inspector can be helpful by providing you with an inspection report. The inspection report gives you a good understanding about the condition of the home. With your inspection report, if there are repairs which need to be made, you as the buyer will be made aware of the required repairs as well as whether the repairs need to be completed prior to the closing. At this point, your Realtor and your attorney may be able to negotiate home repairs on your behalf.

From the point at which time you first applied for your home loan to your closing date, you may need to update your lender by supplying current pay stubs, your most recent bank statements, as well as other pertinent financial documents which evidence that the financial condition you are in when you close matches the financial condition you were in when you applied for your home loan.

Your lender can realistically close your loan within ___________ days of the submission of your loan application. Your home loan provider will review your file while working with you to satisfy outstanding loan conditions. You will need to obtain homeowners insurance. You will also want to do an inspection of the property so as to ensure that repairs which were required to be made prior to the closing have been made.

HUD-certified housing counselors provide home buyer education classes which provide buyers with an overview pertaining to, *a)* the home buying process, *b)* real estate fundamentals, *c)* the real estate sale contract, and *d)* home loan application and approval processes. Understanding each of these steps is important for you as you transition from renter to homeowner.

We hope this outline has helped you by answering some of the questions that frequently come up during the pursuit of homeownership. Please do not hesitate to call or email ____________ if there is any additional information you would like.

Developer Proposal: Affordable Homeownership Initiative

Through this Development Plan, ____________ will increase access to affordable home loans in ____________ neighborhoods.

____________ will establish quarterly goals for home loan approvals which are issued to owner-occupying home buyers whose incomes do not exceed ____________ of HUD Median Income. Quarterly home loan approval data will be supplied to the Office of Affordable Housing evidencing ____________ commitment to increase access to affordable home loans in ____________ .

____________ will deploy a ____________ Neighborhood Home Loan Team and will hire ____________ mortgage loan originators to facilitate increased access to affordable home loans in ____________ .

Home loan approvals coupled to housing affordability, affordability which is aligned with HUD Median Income requirements and Office of Affordable Housing standards, will be monitored by the Developer. Monitoring loan data is the measure through which the Developer's commitment to convey newly-built homes to owner-occupying home buyers affordably will be tracked.

The reporting of home loan data will enable transparency, updates and ongoing governance applicable to Office of Affordable Housing guidelines. Our Program, coupled to good Program governance, will ensure that ____________ percentage of purchasers approved to buy homes in ____________ will have incomes which do not exceed ____________ of HUD Median Income.

As stated, home loan data will be compiled by ______________ and supplied to the Office of Affordable Housing. This data will be supplied to the Office of Affordable Housing each quarter.

A quick read: Interest Rates

When a home buyer applies for their home loan, the buyer has the option of locking into an interest rate. When one finances the acquisition of a new car, the buyer of that new car will lock into an interest rate on the car loan. When one uses a student loan to finance their college education one will lock into an interest rate on their student loan.

Each of the three aforementioned borrowing scenarios do involve interest rates, yet none of the aforementioned three interest rate scenarios involve direct interest rate setting nor do they involve direct interest rates established by the Federal Reserve.

The Federal Reserve does not directly set interest rates that everyday American consumers take on as they finance their college educations, their new automobile purchases or their home purchases. Rather, the Federal Reserve influences the overall supply of money in the United States economy.

The Federal Reserve is then the de facto underlying indirect benchmark in determining how much interest we, banks, and companies pay as we find ways to utilize the supply of money available to us in the United States economy. Thus, the Federal Reserve affects the cost of money in the American economy through the Fed's target rate. By setting their target rate, the Federal Reserve influences rates of interest banks charge one another for their use of borrowed funds on an overnight basis.

So, as the Fed's target rate rises, the rates of interest banks charge each other on an overnight basis thus in turn rises as well. As banks charge each other higher rates of interest for the use of their capital, the pass-through in charges transitions to higher interest rates that consumers pay for goods and services that Americans purchase and finance. Albeit, a new car. Or a new home. Or a college degree.

The federal funds rate…

The federal funds rate is the target interest rate set by the Fed. More specifically, the federal funds rate is established by the Fed's Federal Open Market Committee. The federal funds rate is the rate at which banks borrow (and lend) their excess reserves to other banks overnight.

The Federal Reserve's Federal Open Market Committee establishes the federal funds rate. The federal funds rate is also referred to as the federal funds target rate - *i.e.:* the target rate - or the fed funds rate.

The Federal Open Market Committee consists of five members on the Board of Governors, the Chairman, the Vice Chairman, as well as four regional Federal Reserve Bank presidents. The Federal Open Market Committee partakes in eight meetings each year, with meeting intervals for the Federal Open Market Committee set at five to eight weeks apart.

In essence, the federal funds rate is the interest rate that banks charge each other for use of excess cash that banks have on-hand from their reserves. The term used within this context is *excess* and that is because banks do have *required* reserve *accounts.* And banks do have required reserve *requirements.* Reserve requirements for banks are arrived at through a multiple of the bank's total deposits. The target rate - as is established by the Federal Open Market Committee - is the cost of money paid by commercial banks as banks lend - or borrow - excess bank reserves on an overnight basis. Banks are not to allocate funds from their reserve requirements to lending activities. Banks lend excess funds. Not reserve requirements.

In establishing its target rate, the Federal Open Market Committee takes into account the core inflation rate. In January of 2022, the core inflation rate reached 6%. In December of 2021, the core inflation rate registered at 5.5%. In the United States, the last time the core inflation rate hit at least 6% in a month was August of 1982. At that time, the core inflation rate reached 7.1%. Core inflation averaged 7.4% in 1982.

Starting off at a 6% core inflation rate in January of 2022, it had been potentially foreseeable that the Federal Open Market Committee would consider steady interest rate increases at Federal Open Market Committee meetings. Those would be interest rate increases enacted by the Federal Open Market Committee in their effort to thwart an inflationary cycle in the United States.

The topic of interest rates would be included in any conversation one has which involves the binary subject of inflation. In talking about price increases - *i.e.:* inflation - when one refers to the term "core inflation," one is technically referring to inflation, excluding increases in food and energy costs. That means, as the Federal Open Market Committee establishes its target rate, metrics which are not included in the Committee's inflation assessment would be increases in retail prices that Americans pay at the food store. Neither the Fed's inflation assessment nor the Fed's policy-making decisions technically take into account increases that Americans pay at the gasoline pump.

In considering last year's spike in interest rates, then too in looking to potentially identify a visible cause for these rising interest rates (as we know that food prices and gas prices are not technically included in Federal Open Market Committee evaluations for core inflation) one should also realize that the well-known Consumer Price Index (the CPI) is also not a "measuring stick" used by the Federal Open Market Committee in their evaluation of core inflation. Nor in interest rate policy. Rather, the Fed's analysis - as per core inflation - is predicated on the Fed studying the core personal consumption expenditures price index. *I.e.:* the PCE. The core personal consumption expenditures price index is a measure of prices paid by Americans for their purchases of goods and services, excluding food and energy.

The establishment of interest rates…

Open market operations - *i.e.:* the free market, capital deployment… - are an integral component to the Federal Reserve's process whereby the Fed's federal funds effective rate follows the Fed's federal funds target rate. Open market operations: the purchase of and the sale of securities. More specifically, the purchase of and the sale of securities in the open market by a central bank. Short-term open market operation objectives are established by the Federal Open Market Committee.

Going back to the subject of inflation, as inflation is predictive of interest rate increases, core inflation in the United States on an annual basis had not reached the 3% threshold since 1995. In 2021, America's core inflation rate surpassed 3%...reaching 3.6%.

The 3.6% core inflation felt by Americans in 2021 was the highest core inflation rate since 1992. At that time, the core inflation rate reached 3.7%. As such, Americans are coming *from* an environment consisting of low interest rates and low inflation. Arguably, an ideal economic climate. So, as the United States has not incurred a comparable spike in inflation since the early 1990's and in thinking through interest rates - and interest rate policy - coupled to interest rate policy by the Fed, Americans may very well be entering into a cycle of not only higher inflation but of higher interest rates as well.

Off-Market Properties - Shadow Inventory

Vacant and abandoned properties which are not on the market and which are not listed for sale contribute to "shadow inventory." Properties in foreclosure. Bank REO's. Properties which have not yet been put up for sale by property owners. *Shadow inventory.*

Shadow inventory can affect - even thwart - accurate market reads applicable to housing data. Through an accompanying mirror image, shadow inventory might just then be overlooked, maybe even understated, as viable starting points for conversations about increased access to affordable homeownership in neighborhoods where limited opportunities now exist. Limited opportunities *... or so it may seem.*

Distressed properties make up a noted portion of shadow inventory. Distressed properties sell at lower prices than homes which are sold in good condition. So the sale of a shadow inventory property could drive down area home values. Yet that lower sale price of a shadow inventory property does create an ancillary affordable homeownership opportunity - and a benefit - through the lower sale price. And through that lower sale price, a home buyer could gain affordable access to a shadow inventory property. And to an opportunity to become a homeowner.

Properties in foreclosure. Bank REO's. Shadow inventory. So how about city-owned properties? How about land bank properties? City-owned properties and land bank properties would not necessarily be classified as shadow inventory in the traditional sense. Classifications aside, one upside to a foreclosed property and to a bank REO can also be recognized in a city-owned property and in a land bank property. That upside is, *An opportunity for a home buyer to purchase an affordable home.*

Acquiring city-owned properties and land bank properties can create a nice opportunity for real estate developers as well. Benefits associated with this property-type could be amplified by developers acquiring properties at discounted sale prices. Once acquired by developers, properties can then be rehabbed and/or new homes can be constructed on vacant residential lots. Then, properties can be transitioned back into the market as "performing properties." *And as affordable housing.*

Let's look at Kansas City

When I first wrote about the Land Bank of Kansas City, Missouri, Kansas City's Land Bank had a total of one-hundred seventeen Structure Types. These would be categorized as single-family homes. Furthermore, Kansas City's Land Bank had two-thousand seven-hundred fifty properties which had the property classification of Residential Vacant. *I.e.:* vacant lots

While the 117 single-family Land Bank homes and the 2,750 Land Bank residential vacant lots would not be categorized as traditional shadow inventory, these property types could be suitable for center city real estate development projects. Especially when a center city real estate development project is geared towards affordable housing. Then city-owned and land bank properties could present a real nice option for real estate developers.

Let's look at Newark

A few years ago I wrote a developer proposal which was submitted to the Newark New Jersey Department of Economic and Housing Development in response to a Request For Proposals (RFP). Through the RFP, Newark earmarked over four-hundred residential vacant lots to be developed. These were buildable residential lots. *A nice opportunity for real estate developers.*

While the RFP created an opportunity for real estate developers, the RFP also created a channel through which affordable homeownership opportunities could be brought to Newark. The residential lots included in the RFP were earmarked for new two-family and three-family home builds. Homes which would be built by Designated Developers.

One market-based upside to shadow inventory can be found in matching properties to the provision of affordable housing. When looking at housing affordability, then tracing housing affordability back to shadow inventory, then linking shadow inventory to city-owned properties, and/or to land bank properties, one could arguably correlate acquiring city-owned properties to a viable market-based affordable housing solution.

Shadow inventory, city-owned properties, land banks and affordable homeownership. Kansas City, Missouri, has a land bank. You can also find one of those in St, Louis, Australia, Great Britain, Atlanta, Philadelphia, Argentina, Brazil and Paraguay. Detroit has a land bank too.

"There is no inventory..."

U.S. cities own and/or manage thousands of vacant, abandoned, distressed and non-performing properties. In 2020, Philadelphia had in the range of forty-thousand vacant lots. In 2020, Land Bank of Kansas City, MO, had nearly three-thousand vacant lots. In 2020, Chicago had about thirty-two thousand vacant lots. Vacant residential lots constitute non-performing city-owned properties, some of which could reasonably be - with the right developer proposal written - conveyed to developers, *i.e.:* to designated developers. Developers who in turn improve the properties, then transition the improved properties back to the market as "performing" properties.

Performing properties would qualify as inventory. Realtors list inventory as homes that will be sold. Mortgage loan originators originate home loans which are affixed to inventory. Increased housing inventory is a viable market solution. *A plus on many fronts.*

Focusing on non-performing city-owned properties also creates a unique opportunity for home loan providers to build a home loan origination platform. A home loan origination platform could be based upon providing financing required by home buyers to reposition now non-performing city-owned properties back to the market as affordable homes - *i.e.:* as inventory. Inventory which will then be available to owner-occupying home buyers. Many of whom could be first-time home buyers. Home buyers who may feel they have been shut out of homeownership altogether. Due to a lack of affordability. Due to limited inventory. Due to high home prices. *Elevated home prices (and a lack of affordability) are characteristics of a housing market which has limited inventory.*

Oftentimes city-owned properties can be acquired by designated developers at sale prices which are below market values of comparable properties which are on the market. As such, the acquisition of city-owned properties could be a good channel to focus on for real estate developers. These are real estate transactions. The properties can be transitioned from the city to the developer. These transactions constitute sales of now non-performing properties. Properties which do not now generate property tax revenue for a city. Sold to new owners. *Conveyed to designated developers.*

Unimproved, vacant, distressed and non-performing properties create a strain on city budgets: *a)* no revenue coming in coupled to, *b)* money spent by the city managing non-performing properties. Limited money coming in by way of reduced property tax revenues, coupled to money going out. Designated developers could be a windfall for cities. *A solution.*

According to a report organized by SEIU, the Foreclosure Crisis is estimated to have cost the City of Newark nearly $2 trillion in lost property tax revenue. A revenue loss of $2,000,000,000,000 (12 zeros) would strain *any* city's budget. Newark determined that the utilization of property auctions could serve as a means by which the City's deficit could be paid down by selling non-performing properties at auctions.

In some years, Newark City Council budgets included stipulations whereby the State of New Jersey could (ideally) permit Newark to reduce its required contribution into the City's reserve for uncollected property taxes. A reserve is a fund that states require municipalities to contribute to in order to make up for uncollected taxes from the year prior. Past Newark budgets included projections totaling upwards of $40,000,000 - projected revenue inbound to Newark - coming through sales of city-owned properties.

A hollowing out of any city's property tax base requires the rebuilding of that same hollowed out property tax base. *It's new home construction.* This being said, the process whereby an owner-occupying home buyer secures a construction loan can be daunting. Furthermore, a Realtor will be paid when a home buyer selects a property to purchase through the MLS. Clear, understandable and quick…yet not necessarily the process which makes up new home construction and city-owned properties.

The underwriting of construction loans can be highly-detailed and stringent, complete with potential delays; delays in the mortgage loan originator who originated the construction loan getting paid. Potential loan officer payday delays, attributed to, focusing loan origination sales efforts on new home construction.

With new home builds, architectural renderings need to be obtained, paid for, and then approved by the city in order for a buyer's proposed home build to move forward. The home buyer - and the home buyer's Realtor - need to navigate new home construction.

Loan officers would probably prefer it when a loan they originate is easier, and delivered to them. *Close in 30 days* is a good scenario for mortgage loan originator paydays. Quick paydays are not necessarily in line for loan officers who focus on new home construction.

In order for an owner-occupying home buyer to build a new home, that home buyer's home builder would need to first be approved by the home buyer's bank. Builder approval by the bank is among a plethora of things that need to happen with new home construction. Lots of things need to go very right. It's complicated, lengthy and involved. So, short-termism could prevent viable market solutions from taking hold. *"Short-term" is just not new home construction.*

In Newark (or Philadelphia, or Chicago, or Kansas City) depressed property values in underserved neighborhoods which have high numbers of vacant and unimproved properties could mean that a homeowner's newly-built home will have an appraisal which comes in at a value which is less than the cost-to-build the home. *A challenge.*

With the traditional home buying process, busy families just do not have experience dealing with architects. So in Newark, for example, City officials took good steps to provide a menu of renderings which could be made available to prospective home buyers. The renderings wisely included several distinct home designs. This was a well thought-out solution. Yet the challenge still being, *The cost of construction for a new home build could exceed neighborhood home values.* This is a legitimate challenge when it comes to securing financing for the new home build. Even when the home buyer and their Realtor successfully navigate: *a)* getting architectural plans, *b)* getting the home builder approved with the bank providing the financing, and *c)* obtaining permits and approvals.

Then what if, with some down time, a prospective Newark home buyer goes onto ZILLOW? In doing so, a prospective home buyer (and/or a home loan provider) might determine that in some years, it had been projected that nearly twenty-five percent of homes in Newark had negative equity. Whereby the national average is less than 10%. Opinions could be formed. Maybe a barrier could be formed in terms of the buyer continuing to want to buy the home or for the home loan provider to want to provide a home loan to the buyer so they can purchase the home. Each, a potential obstacle which could take hold.

Going back a few years, according to ZILLOW, the median sale price of a Newark home, as of November 30, 2019 was $228,400. At that same time, in the Fairmount neighborhood of Newark, the median home value was $193,300. In the University Heights neighborhood? $160,400. The West Side neighborhood? $177,300. Those home values could be less than the cost to build a new construction home. Less than the cost to build a new home in these very same neighborhoods. This is a potential challenge with new home construction.

There can be challenges with comparable home sales (and home values) when taking on new home construction projects in urban centers. Yet, one can see how this challenge could *potentially* begin to solve itself.

Real estate could first be looked at as a home, not primarily as a "financial instrument." Newark could be adopted as the home buyer's neighborhood, not as a place where prioritizing short term home equity increases is so relevant. *It's all in how one looks at what a home really is.*

Using a real life example, I am from New Jersey zip code 07046 and I lived for fourteen years in Kansas - zip code 66801. When you Google each zip code, 07046 "wins," except for the fact that I had a nicer home, made better friends, found a more welcoming community, and have far more fond memories in zip code 66801. As Bruce Marks, CEO of Neighborhood Assistance Corporation of America once told me, *"There are different forms of currency."*

Through my own submission of developer proposals in Newark, I have really enjoyed meeting some of the most wonderful people. Some of the kindest people I have met in real estate are involved in transitioning Newark city-owned properties to developers. Newark is filled with very real "currency." Yet there is no specific ZILLOW category for this valuation type, nor for this currency type.

The financialization of homeownership is one barrier to the solution, in my humble opinion. Looking at real estate as an asset, rather than as a home, could be one challenge. Looking at real estate as an "ATM machine." Looking at real estate as a way to cash-out on the home's equity. Looking at the real estate, and somehow thinking that a school district in an isolated homogeneous suburb is the only way to *"make our kids smart."* Each could be potential barriers to substantive gains attained through center city redevelopment. These are challenges to a solution. Just as socioeconomics played a role in how cities were hollowed out in the first place, socioeconomic factors are a reason for why there continue to be high numbers of abandoned, non-performing and vacant properties in city centers. Reaching a different set of socioeconomic viewpoints altogether could be one way to overcome some of the barriers that prevent transitioning vacant non-performing city-owned properties back to the market as "performing" properties. To families. And doing so, *affordably.*

Between 2000 and 2006 the number of building permits issued in Newark tripled. During this same time period, the increase in permits issued was in large part driven by real estate investors. Real estate investors often have teams in place to build new homes and to finance those new home builds.

Numbers of building permits issued could be projected to increase substantially in cities which have elevated levels of vacant, unimproved lots. *One might assume.* Real estate investors were instrumental in increases in the number of building permits issued in Newark. It's about *teams.* Organized teams. Specialized teams. Individual owner-occupying home buying families in Newark (or Chicago, or Kansas City, or Philadelphia) simply oftentimes just do not have these teams available to them. However, a real estate professional could build such a team. So too could a mortgage loan originator.

Looking at how mortgage companies and at how real estate offices are very much in the business of building sales teams, a focused home loan provider and/or a focused real estate professional could effectively integrate the following services while standing out in the market by doing so:

a) Providing low down payment affordable home loans.
b) Specializing in the acquisition of city-owned properties.
c) The implementation of a Program for owner-occupying home buyers which

enables buyers to acquire city-owned properties and to finance new home builds. *d)* Specializing in the provision of down payment assistance programs which can be made available to first-time home buyers.

Looking at Opportunity Zones: Kansas City

Kansas City, Missouri, was one of the most aggressive U.S. cities when it came to attracting Opportunity Zone projects. In Kansas City, MO, Opportunity Zone projects were viewed by many as potential catalysts for continued Kansas City, MO, neighborhood revitalization. Furthermore, in Kansas City, *18th and Vine, 31st and Troost, Prospect, Ivanhoe* and the *Westside Neighborhood* were categorized to be priority areas under the Kansas City Catalytic Urban Redevelopment Initiative.

Kansas City, MO, utilized a four-tiered approach with Opportunity Zones: *1)* community development, *2)* local business growth, *3)* workforce development, and *4)* utilization of public and private capital. Yet, a challenge still remained. KCMO neighborhood stakeholders often lacked access to financing vehicles needed in order to participate in Opportunity Zone projects. Be they real estate projects, be they business start-ups, or be it the expansion of existing businesses. *Access to financing is key.*

According to a study conducted by the Kauffman Foundation, a significant portion of entrepreneurs in Kansas City lack access to bank financing, thus stripping entrepreneurs of necessary venture capital. In Kansas City, as is the case in any city for that matter, financing is required.

While access to financing is needed in order to fund a startup - as well as to fund ongoing business operations for that start-up - access to financing is also required by non-business owners who live in Kansas City, MO, Opportunity Zones. These would be non-business owners who come in the form of prospective owner-occupying Kansas City home buyers…Kansas Citians who would like to buy, to rehab, and to then live in what may now be a non-performing center city Kansas City, MO, home which happens to be located in a Kansas City, MO, Opportunity Zone. And to live in the home once it has been rehabbed.

Without access to affordable homes and financing, Opportunity Zone neighborhood stakeholders - those who live in Kansas City, MO, Opportunity Zones now - could end up receiving fewer of the benefits available to those participating in KCMO Opportunity Zone real estate development.

Relocation by start-ups and mature businesses to Kansas City, MO, Opportunity Zones, along with the development of home grown Kansas City, MO, Opportunity Zone start-up businesses each serve as a catalyst for Kansas City, MO, neighborhood revitalization. And to the growth of mixed-use center city Kansas City, MO, communities. Each leading to higher rates of homeownership, to higher neighborhood home values and to increased interest among banks in providing loans to home buyers in now-underserved Kansas City, MO, neighborhoods. Increased home equity, by way of higher home values - the result of new home construction and the rehabbing of homes - creates opportunities for Kansas City, MO, neighborhood stakeholders to use newfound home equity to fund start-up businesses.

Looking at what could arguably be Kansas City's most famous neighborhood - the 18th and Vine Jazz District - the designation of the 18th and Vine Jazz District as an Opportunity Zone created investor interest in housing and real estate projects in 18th and Vine. Less investor interest had been shown in financing startup businesses, or in funding the relocation and/or the expansion of existing businesses in 18th and Vine. Real estate investor focus in 18th and Vine dominated the landscape when it came to Opportunity Zone projects. *And the acquisition of real estate requires financing.*

31st and Troost Avenue in Midtown Kansas City, MO, once rivaled KC's Country Club Plaza as a Kansas City hot spot. 31st and Troost had once been a thriving shopping and entertainment district. Years of underinvestment coupled to challenging socioeconomic factors took their toll on 31st and Troost. This being said, one development project which had been slated for the 31st and Troost district included bringing twenty-eight market rate rental apartments as well as 85,000 square feet of commercial space to the 31st and Troost neighborhood. *A planned $18,000,000 Opportunity Zone project.*

Benefits flowed to Kansas City, MO, and to KCMO investors thanks to the roll out of Opportunity Zones. 31st and Troost is one such example. Yet, looking at 18th and Vine, one proposed approach could be to think through coupling real estate benefits in Kansas City, MO, coming by way of Opportunity Zone investments to the idea behind the establishment of Empowerment Zones. Which in Kansas City, MO, has a state comparable. *A Missouri equivalent.*

Empowerment Zones

Empowerment Zones came about during the Clinton Administration as a result of the Empowerment Zones and Enterprise Communities Act of 1993. Empowerment Zones focus on people and on local services, not just on capital investments.

Empowerment Zones encourage hiring. Empowerment Zones put into place subsidies for up-front investment in capital and equipment, with an eye on how deployed subsidies could enhance hiring patterns. Empowerment Zones provide for loan guarantees and can be accompanied by regulatory waivers. Empowerment Zones enable local governments to receive grants for local services and infrastructure. Similar to Opportunity Zones, Empowerment Zones can lead to preferential tax treatment.

While Kansas City, MO, would not be located in an Empowerment Zone (St. Louis, MO, is), in Kansas City, MO, one idea could be to couple interest in Opportunity Zone real estate projects to advantages available to Kansas City, MO, start-ups - and to Kansas City, MO, existing businesses - located in a Missouri Enhanced Enterprise Zone.

Missouri Enhanced Enterprise Zones (EEZ) could be created by local communities. The focus in an EEZ is job creation in blighted areas. Local incentives may be available to businesses that expand operations in Enhanced Enterprise Zones. In Kansas City, MO, the Midtown area, south to the former Richards-Gebaur Memorial Airport, falls within an Enhanced Enterprise Zone.

Affordable housing: Developers and banks face challenges. Structural solutions exist in the market, thanks to HUD

The process whereby developers identify vacant land on which they can profitably build homes in neighborhoods which are being gentrified has long been cited as one obstacle to increasing access to affordable housing. Then, would a developer even build affordable housing when homeownership is difficult to attain in neighborhoods where a disproportionately high percentage of prospective home buyers have "very-low" incomes as measured by HUD? "Very low" would denote an income at or below 50% of area HUD Median Income. Lower credit scores in blighted neighborhoods could further exacerbate the challenge. Then there's this approach: *How about focusing on increasing access to affordable home loans in underserved neighborhoods?*

A mortgage loan originator might have a genuine lack of interest in originating home loans with smaller loan balances in urban neighborhoods. It could be, in all probability, less profitable for a mortgage loan originator to originate a smaller home loan in say, a blighted urban neighborhood, than it would be for that same mortgage loan originator to originate a larger loan, in say, a suburban neighborhood which does not suffer from disinvestment. Nor from blight. The suburban neighborhood's higher home values could lead to increased profitability for the mortgage loan originator in comparison to originating home loans with smaller loan balances in underserved neighborhoods. Add in the additional time required of the mortgage loan originator to work with prospective home buyers who might have credit challenges and who need access to down payment assistance programs. All things considered, it's just plain old harder work for the mortgage loan originator. *Maybe for less pay.*

While tax abatements, political will, home buyer education courses, access to down payment assistance programs, city issuances of RFP's/RFQ's for real estate developers and leadership/vision/entrepreneurial thinking in board rooms at banks can assuage some of these barriers, challenges still remain when it comes to building quality affordable homes in blighted urban neighborhoods. It is oftentimes rather difficult to increase access to affordable home loans in underserved neighborhoods.

The FHA and Opportunity Zones

The FHA established incentives for property owners who invest in Opportunity Zones include, *a)* lower costs, and *b)* dedicated underwriters. Three HUD programs - *1)* Section 207/223(f), *2)* Section 220, and *3)* Section 221(d)(4) - were eligible for Multifamily Accelerated Processing (MAP).

• Section 207/223(f): Mortgage insurance for the purchase or the refinancing of existing multi-family rental housing.
• Section 220: Mortgage insurance for rental housing for urban renewal and concentrated development areas.
• Section 221(d)(4): Mortgage insurance for rental and cooperative housing.

"If you are doing a project within an Opportunity Zone and you are applying for one of our grants, you get some preference. So that, along with the tax advantages, will drive people to look at those (areas). We are also offering very specific technical assistance to help them coordinate their efforts." - Ben Carson, the then-Secretary of HUD, in an interview with *The Real Deal* in March 2019.

Mortgage Insurance for Rental and Cooperative Housing: Section 221(d)(4) - Section 221(d)(4) insures mortgage loans used to facilitate new construction or substantial rehabilitation of multifamily rental or cooperative housing for moderate-income families, the elderly and the handicapped. Single Room Occupancy (SRO) projects may also be insured under this section. Section 221(d)(4) insures lenders against loss on mortgage defaults. Section 221(d)(4) assists the private industry with the construction or the rehabilitation of rental and cooperative housing for moderate-income and displaced families by making capital more readily available. The program allows for long-term mortgages (up to 40 years) that can be financed through Government National Mortgage Association (GNMA) Mortgage Backed Securities.

FHA mortgage insurance for HUD-approved lenders - Insured mortgages which can be used to finance the construction or the rehabilitation of detached, semi-detached, row, walkup or elevator-type rental or cooperative housing containing five or more units. The program has statutory mortgage limits which vary according to the size of the unit, the type of structure and the location of the project. Families are eligible to occupy dwellings in a structure where the mortgage is insured within the parameters of the FHA, subject to approved tenant selection. There are no income limits. Projects may be designed specifically for the elderly or handicapped.

Section 221(d)(4) - Multifamily Accelerated Processing (MAP). Sponsors work with MAP-approved lenders who submit required exhibits for the pre-application stage. HUD reviews the lender's exhibits and will either invite the lender to apply for a firm commitment for mortgage insurance or decline to consider the application further. If HUD determines that the exhibits are acceptable the lender then submits the firm commitment application - including a full underwriting package - to the local Multifamily Hub or Program Center for review. The application is reviewed to determine whether the proposed loan is an acceptable risk. Considerations include market need, zoning, architectural merits, capabilities of the borrower and availability of community resources, etc. If the proposed project meets program requirements, the local Multifamily Hub or Program Center issues a commitment to the lender for mortgage insurance.

Applications submitted by non-MAP lenders must be processed by HUD field office staff under Traditional Application Processing (TAP). The sponsor has a pre-application conference with the local HUD Multifamily Hub or Program Center to determine the preliminary feasibility of the project. The sponsor must then submit a site appraisal and market analysis (SAMA) application (for new construction projects) or a feasibility application (for substantial rehabilitation projects). Following HUD's issuance of a SAMA or a feasibility letter, the sponsor then submits the firm commitment application through a HUD-approved lender for processing. If the proposed project meets program requirements, the local Multifamily Hub or Program Center issues a commitment to the lender for mortgage insurance.

The 221(d)(4) program - National Housing Act (12 U.S.C. 17151 (d)(4). Program regulations are found at 24 CFR 221, subparts C and D. Basic TAP program instructions are in HUD handbook 4560.01 - Mortgage Insurance for Multifamily Moderate Income Housing Projects are available on HUDclips. Refer to the MAP web-site for guidelines and instructions, lender approval requirements and MAP coordinators. The program is administered by the Office of Multifamily Housing Programs, Office of Production, Program Administration Division.

Program Accomplishments: In Fiscal year 2015 the Department insured mortgages for one-hundred ninety-two projects with 30,412 units. All total? *A $2.9 billion allocation of capital.*

Mortgage Insurance for the Purchase or the Refinancing of Existing Multifamily Rental Housing Section 207/223(F) - Section 207/223(f) insures mortgage loans to facilitate the purchase or the refinancing of existing multifamily rental housing. Projects may have been financed originally with either conventional or FHA insured mortgages. Properties requiring substantial rehabilitation are not eligible for mortgage insurance under this program. HUD requires the completion of critical repairs before endorsement of the mortgage and permits the completion of non-critical repairs after the endorsement for mortgage insurance.

Section 223(f) insures lenders against loss on mortgage defaults. The program allows for long-term mortgages (up to 35 years) that can be financed with Government National Mortgage Association (GNMA) mortgage-backed securities.

Eligibility for purchase in the secondary market improves the availability of loan funds and permits more favorable interest rates.

Type of Assistance: FHA mortgage insurance for HUD-approved lenders/eligible activities - The property must contain at least five residential units with complete kitchens and baths and must have been completed or substantially rehabilitated at least three years prior to the date of the application for mortgage insurance. The program allows for non-critical repairs that must be completed within twelve months of loan closing. Projects requiring substantial rehabilitation are not acceptable under this section and may not involve the replacement of more than one major system. The remaining economic life of the project must be long enough to permit a ten-year mortgage. The mortgage term cannot exceed thirty-five years or seventy-five percent of the estimated life of the physical improvements, whichever is less. Prevailing wage requirements do not apply to this program.

Data provided below represent the applicable percentages for estimated values of properties after completion of repairs and/or home improvements.

90% for Section 202 & 202/8 Direct Loans
87% for projects with 90% or greater rental assistance
85% for projects that meet the definition of Affordable Housing
83.3% for market rate projects

Eligible borrowers consist of both for-profit and non-profit applicants. Eligible applicants are persons who are eligible to occupy such projects, subject to normal occupancy restrictions.

Section 223(f) is eligible for Multifamily Accelerated Processing (MAP) - The sponsor works with the MAP-approved lender who then submits required exhibits for a firm commitment application. This includes a full underwriting package which will be submitted to the local Multifamily Hub or Program Center for review. The Multifamily Hub or Program Center reviews the application to determine whether the proposed loan is an acceptable risk. Considerations include, *a)* market need, and *b)* capabilities of the borrower. The FHA underwriting analysis must determine that there is enough project income to repay the loan while taking into account necessary project expenses. If the proposed project meets program requirements, the local Multifamily Hub or Program Center issues a commitment to the lender for mortgage insurance.

Applications submitted by non-MAP lenders must be processed by HUD field office staff under Traditional Application Processing (TAP). Under TAP, there are only two processing stages: *1)* the conditional commitment stage, and *2)* the firm commitment stage. The sponsor is required to have a pre-application conference during the conditional commitment stage to determine the appraised value and the maximum mortgage amount. At the firm commitment stage the local HUD Multifamily Hub or Program Center determines the amount of the mortgage available to the purchaser - or to the refinancing borrower - in the proposed transaction. If the proposal meets FHA program requirements, the local Multifamily Hub or Program Center issues a commitment to the lender for mortgage insurance. Section 223(f) of the National Housing Act was added by Section 311(a) of the Housing and Community Development Act of 1974.

In fiscal year 2015, the Department insured mortgages for five-hundred projects with 70,142 units. The total? *$4.5 billion.*

HUD is a catalyst to affordable housing development

In February of 2019, the FHA's low-income housing tax credit financing pilot program was expanded to incorporate projects in Opportunity Zones. Through a collaborative effort, federal agencies worked together with HUD to coordinate their efforts in a manner which was focused on extending Opportunity Zone tax benefits to developers.

Applicable to Opportunity Zone grants, former HUD Secretary Ben Carson positioned the agency to give a preference to real estate developers who planned to undertake affordable housing projects located within Opportunity Zones. The effort was inclusive of HUD's "macro-directive," so-to-speak, which had been undertaken by then-Secretary Carson to create interest among investors, Wall Street and developers in affordable housing projects in Opportunity Zones. *Why so?*

Opportunity Zone projects do not specifically require affordable housing construction. There is no Opportunity Zone affordable housing mandate. So, catalysts were put into place through HUD to get *"...affordable housing shovels in the ground"* within Opportunity Zones. Thus creating more interest in Opportunity Zone-directed affordable housing development at the national level.

Furthermore, HUD backed initiatives at local levels to drive targeted affordable housing development. An example of this was found in efforts by HUD to encourage cities to amend local zoning regulations to favor affordable housing development.

"If you are doing a project within an Opportunity Zone and you are applying for one of our grants, you get some preference. So that, along with the tax advantages, will drive people to look at those (areas). We are also offering very specific technical assistance to help them coordinate their efforts." - then-HUD Secretary Ben Carson

By 2020, over 600,000 FHA home loans were secured by properties located in Opportunity Zones.

Thinking through Opportunity Zones, potentially coupled to mortgage loan origination revenue, banks, mortgage companies, mortgage brokers and mortgage bankers had a unique opportunity at-hand.

By paying attention to Opportunity Zones, an aspiring home loan provider could develop their own unique loan origination platform within Opportunity Zones by focusing efforts on benefits available to existing homeowners and prospective home buyers, then coupling homeowner benefits to the market and to home loan origination "tools."

Opportunity Zones covered more than 8,700 United States census tracts. All fifty states in the United States established Opportunity Zones. An Opportunity Zone was categorized as an economically-distressed community. A neighborhood where new investments under certain conditions could be eligible for preferential treatment. Looking at three states alone - Missouri, New Jersey and Pennsylvania - there were six-hundred thirty Opportunity Zones. Missouri had one-hundred sixty-one designated Opportunity Zones. New Jersey had one-hundred sixty-nine designated Opportunity Zones. Pennsylvania had three-hundred designated Opportunity Zones. *In 2020, there were eighty-two Opportunity Zones in Philadelphia alone.*

So how about an "Opportunity Zone Home Loan Origination Business?" What would that look like? First comes the product. The products (plural) were put into place for the mortgage loan originator, available through Fannie Mae, Freddie Mac and HUD. A mortgage loan originator could utilize these "loan tools" which were put into place and sitting in the mortgage loan originator's "tool shed." Among these "tools" would be, *a)* the Fannie Mae HomeStyle Renovation loan, *b)* the Freddie Mac CHOICERenovation loan, and *c)* the FHA 203(k) loan.

Let's look at the FHA 203(k)...

The Limited 203(k) loan is intended to be used to improve a home's functionality while also improving the overall attractiveness of the home. New flooring, roof repairs, the elimination of health and safety hazards (for example, lead-based paint stabilization), new plumbing, HVAC and electrical systems, connection to public water and sewage systems as well as energy conservation improvements. These are a few of the eligible home improvements available to a homeowner - and/or to a prospective home buyer - as per their utilization of the FHA 203(k) loan.

Whereas 203(k) home improvements had once been capped at $35,000, HUD later increased this $35,000 home improvement cap to $50,000. The FHA loan amount increase - from $35,000 to $50,000 - applied to the first 15,000 FHA 203(k) loans each calendar year.

A mortgage loan originator might not necessarily think about new sewer lines, improving neighborhoods, the 2017 Tax Cuts and Jobs Act, land banks, electrical systems, Opportunity Zones or stabilizing communities for that matter, when they are thinking through their home loan origination goals. Nor when they are strategizing to win company-sponsored home loan origination contests. This being said, a mortgage loan originator might think about originating more FHA loans. Then think about linking FHA home loan origination sales goals to the market. Then coupling this to a specific loan origination strategy. *Then to Opportunity Zones.*

A proposed gameplan: How about FHA home loans in Opportunity Zones?

In 2020, it had been reported that there were over 620,000 active FHA-insured mortgages secured by eligible properties within qualified Opportunity Zones. The 620,000-plus active FHA loans represented just about eight percent of the total number of FHA loans in place and active, nationally, at that time.

The FHA 203(k) enables the home buyer to acquire and rehab a home. A home which may be in an older neighborhood. Quite possibly, a home which is located within an Opportunity Zone. A distressed home that needs some "TLC." In this regard, the FHA 203(k) loan could be a facilitator for more purchase business for the mortgage loan originator. The FHA 203(k) loan also creates another great opportunity for the mortgage professional as well: *Refinances in an Opportunity Zone.*

The Limited 203(k) allows an existing homeowner to finance repairs and home improvements made to their primary residence, *i.e.:* the home they already own, the home they live in now. The Limited 203(k) could facilitate a home remodeling project for the homeowner who already has an FHA loan. For their home, which happens to be located in one of the 8,700 census tracts in Opportunity Zones. A product-specific focus such as this, implemented by the mortgage loan originator, could be developed to create an expansive loan origination platform. A platform focused on refinances in Opportunity Zones. There were those 620,000-plus FHA mortgages secured by properties located in Opportunity Zones. This could create a nice opportunity for refinance business for mortgage lenders.

Within neighborhoods in which FHA 203(k) home loans will be originated, would there likely be a focus by real estate investors? How about new home buyers? A neighbor interested in rehabbing a home for themselves, maybe? How about community organizations? Media interest? And Realtors would be prospecting in those neighborhoods too, wouldn't they? Each of whom, any of whom, or maybe even all of whom could be considered to be ideal referral sources - value-adding business relationships - along with being individuals interested in learning about the *Opportunity Zone Home Loan Origination Business* developed by the loan officer. A business relationship cultivated, and a business plan written up.

Over coffee. Maybe on a laptop. In a notebook with sketches. Maybe at a Starbucks somewhere in Philadelphia. Or in Kansas City (at the Filling Station, if in KC). Thought through when asking oneself this question: *How can I win the home loan origination contest for my company?*

Developers often look for (and find) opportunities in non-performing homes

Possibilities to consider when thinking through how to transition vacant, abandoned, non-performing properties from absentee owners to developers, then to owner-occupying home buyers might include:

a) Land banks
b) Spot blight eminent domain
c) Receivership

Why focus on this challenge? Why focus on proposing workable solutions?

Elevated neighborhood vacancy rates correlate to quantifiable financial costs for municipalities. There are so many of these to speak to. To pick just one, how about the cost of demolishing an abandoned single-family home? Demolition can cost a city thousands of dollars with every home demolished.

Then there are social costs too. Neighborhoods with high vacancy rates can become "breeding grounds" for crime, for drug use and for violence. These are a few of the social costs which often accompany high concentrations of non-performing homes in neighborhoods. But social costs are sometimes not able to be quantified by dollars and cents. Sadly, social costs could sometimes be viewed as, *Someone else's problem...not mine.* But are social costs really someone else's problem?

Social costs attributed to high neighborhood vacancy rates correlate to quantifiable financial costs. Financial costs incurred by a city. Financial costs incurred by city stakeholders. Financial costs incurred by city taxpayers. Social costs attributed to high neighborhood vacancy rates are linked to that very same city resident who may not think, at first, that this problem of vacant and abandoned properties is not their problem. *But it is.*

For example, a New Yorker doing very well in life, living maybe in Tribeca. Or maybe living on the Upper East Side. They are still part of New York City. As such, they pay taxes. So, while life may be pretty good for them, and while maybe there are few observable social costs in their own "backyard," the Tribeca neighborhood resident is still linked to their fellow New Yorker who lives in, say, the poorest neighborhood in New York City. Say, the Morrisania neighborhood in the Bronx. Or, maybe the Crotona neighborhood in the Bronx. In Morrisania and Crotona, upwards of forty percent of residents are reported to be living below the federal poverty level.

Let's just say, socioeconomic challenges in Morrisania or Crotona cause some homeowners to enter into foreclosure. A foreclosure could lead to an abandoned home, to a vacant home, then to increased neighborhood police patrolling as one byproduct of elevated vacancy rates. *I.e.:* efforts taken to circumvent the spiraling of adverse circumstances which could lead to a neighborhood becoming a high-crime neighborhood. Addressing non-performing neighborhood properties is, I would argue, a challenge which is in everyone's best interest to think about, be they of ample means or be they of modest means.

Increased police patrolling is a financial cost; a financial cost which addresses the social cost. And it's a City cost. Not just a Morrisania cost. Not just a Crotona cost.

Numerous studies support the premise that city blocks with high numbers of vacant and abandoned properties have crime rates which can be up to twice as high as crime rates on city blocks which do not have comparable numbers of vacant and abandoned properties.

In 2011 the Federal Reserve Bank in Kansas City reported that one in ten residential properties in Kansas City, Missouri, was vacant. That ratio increased to one in four properties within certain afflicted KCMO neighborhoods. According to one Kansas City Star article, at around that same time, there were estimated to have been between 10,000 and 11,000 vacant homes in Kansas City, Missouri.

How about the social costs?

A significant number of Kansas City, MO, homicides have disproportionately occurred within one 34-square mile radius of KCMO. Furthermore, according to Kansas City Police Department data, 75% of KCMO homicides between 2011 through 2014 took place within this same 34-square mile area, a section of the city in which a disproportionately high number of vacant, distressed and non-performing properties were located. Between 2015 and 2018, just about six out of ten Kansas City, Missouri, homicides took place within KCMO's urban core, this being the same urban core which would also have a high portion of the city's vacant and abandoned properties.

A "healthy" homeowner vacancy rate for a city is often considered to be 2% or lower. A "healthy" rental vacancy rate for a city is often considered to be between 7% to 8%. A vacancy rate in excess of 12% is considered to be "high vacancy," whereas a vacancy rate above 20% is categorized as "hyper-vacancy."

While vacant and abandoned properties is a nationwide challenge, there are different characteristics attributed to this challenge, city-by-city. For example, Baltimore's vacant housing problem tends to run throughout the city. The challenge in Baltimore spreads to the outlying areas of Baltimore's boundaries as well.

In 2010, Baltimore had in excess of 16,000 vacant buildings. Fast forward to 2018, eight years later and tens of millions of dollars had been spent to address issues related to blight in Baltimore. All the while, that number - 16,000 vacant, non-performing properties - remained constant.

How about Detroit? Hyper-vacancy remains a major problem in Detroit, citywide. According to Data Driven Detroit, as a city, Detroit at one time had in excess of 40,000 vacant homes. Nearly seventy percent of Detroit's vacant homes had at one time been owned by Detroit Land Bank Authority.

According to one report, Detroit had in the range of 70,000 abandoned buildings, upwards of 30,000 empty houses, *plus 90,000 vacant lots.*

Vacant and abandoned properties represent a nationwide challenge. Yet, in my humble opinion, it's the "macro" which could facilitate a "micro" solution. The "micro" in this discussion being the building of businesses which are focused on providing proposed solutions to a city's vacant and abandoned housing problem. To do so, a practitioner needs, *1)* "tools," and *2)* a "toolkit."

So, invert the "lens to this camera" for a moment, so-to-speak. In doing so, one may now see a nationwide opportunity for real estate developers. And as such, maybe then circle back to an earlier point made in this book: *Processes to consider when thinking through how to transition vacant and abandoned properties from absentee owners to developers, then to owner-occupying home buyers.* And this might include, *a) land banking, b) spot blight eminent domain,* and *c) receivership.*

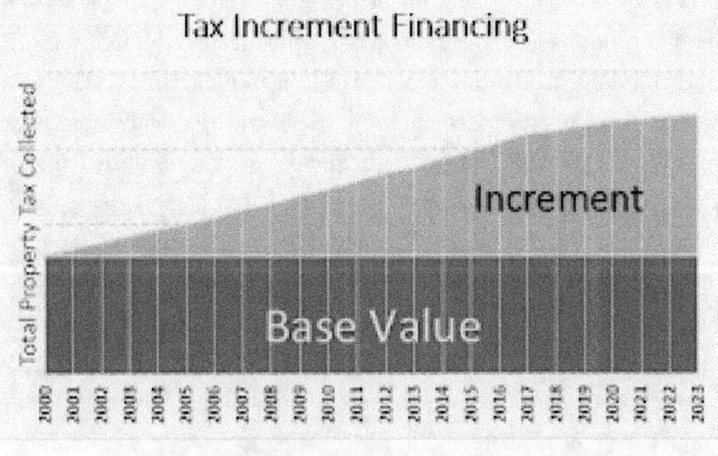

Tax Incremental Financing (TIF)

When considering whether to pursue a real estate development project in an Opportunity Zone, involving local government officials in discussions about the potential availability of tax incremental financing (TIF) is one early step for a real estate developer to consider. Tax incremental financing is in essence a development subsidy, one where a municipality diverts future tax revenue towards economic development. The origin of TIF goes back to the State of California and to 1952. In order to establish the TIF subsidy, an urban renewal district - a TIF district - is first drawn up by a municipality. By creating the TIF district, borrowing capacity is thus established within that TIF district for future real estate development projects. One trade-off being the municipality diverts increases in future real estate tax revenue away from parcels within the TIF district. Property tax revenue is diverted away from the municipality and towards real estate development. *It's a real estate development subsidy.* This diversion of property taxes away from the municipality - and out of the local budget - would go on for say, twenty or twenty-five years.

One idea behind TIF is that real estate development can increase property values, and not only within the TIF district. But also in surrounding areas. As the argument goes, increased area property values could offset TIF subsidies because increased property values create additional property tax revenue for the municipality through increased real estate development within the TIF district.

Furthermore, it is a widely-held belief that one byproduct which accompanies urban revitalization is gentrification. While gentrification does alter the "DNA" within urban cores, gentrification can also lead to higher real estate values; to higher values of properties located within a TIF district, and to an increase in property tax revenue collected by the municipality as a result of increased real estate development. Higher property values coupled to an increase in property tax revenue can serve as a nice financial windfall for municipalities.

And then there is the, *People's homes are just worth more money...* Both in surrounding areas and within the TIF district itself. This leads to additional increases in property tax revenue for the municipality. The result? Higher real estate values in an urban core and in surrounding areas. *Reinforcing the premise for use of TIF.*

But does the establishment of TIF and of a TIF district necessarily serve neighborhood members within that TIF district? For this to occur, TIF could be paired to the designation of an urban area as "blighted."

This designation of "blight" is a key component to TIF, in my humble opinion. This is so because designating an area as "blighted" enables a municipality to acquire private property for public use through eminent domain. Yet the subject of eminent domain might not be a politically tenable talking point to include in campaign speeches for aspiring politicians.

An irony about TIF can be found in the very state where TIF originated - California. In 2011, then-California Governor Jerry Brown enacted legislation which led to the elimination of over four-hundred California redevelopment agencies. While California RDA's played an important role in urban revitalization since their formation in 1945, then-Governor Brown's legislation, coupled to a 6-1 California Supreme Court ruling, ended RDA's in California.

In California, the RDA's that then-Governor Brown eliminated also eliminated TIF. Thus in turn altering proposed real estate development projects in California as a result of the absence of TIF. With the elimination of California RDA's, TIF was no longer a "tool" used to redevelop "blighted" urban neighborhoods.

Reconciling circumstances: *a)* there are benefits to TIF, *b)* RDA's played an important role in revitalization efforts in California, *c)* RDA's in California were eliminated, *d)* the new national "pathways" to real estate development *could be Opportunity Zones.*

So the State of California would seemingly be fertile ground for real estate developers to establish non-governmental private market redevelopment entities, transitioning reliance away from TIF to real estate development projects that can be undertaken by developers. Developers with a newfound focus placed upon Opportunity Zone development projects in California could then pair, *1)* responses submitted to RFP's/RFQ's, *2)* developer proposals, *3)* increased access to affordable home loans which are made available within neighborhoods where gentrification is taking place, and *4)* Opportunity Zone development projects.

Developer Proposals can function as catalysts to increased opportunities within blighted neighborhoods. These newfound opportunities within blighted neighborhoods extend beyond housing.

We can use the sample Developer Proposal below as an example for how a real estate developer might consider approaching a municipality with the goal being to acquire city-owned properties, while also serving as a catalyst to increases in local employment opportunities.

Sample: Developer Proposal

One byproduct of the __________ Developer Proposal will be increased access to affordable home loans in ____________ . Our home loan origination platform will increase access to low down payment FHA home loans in ____________ while leading to the hiring of mortgage loan originators who will participate in __________ Training Program. Our Training Program will cover, *1)* providing new hires with an overview for their career as a ____________ mortgage loan originator, *2)* a discussion of licensing requirements.

Company training:
1. The __________ Training Program is a two-day/sixtccn hour Program.
2. Newly-hired mortgage loan originators will work under experienced mortgage professionals in our Mentorship Program.
3. Underwriting positions with __________ will be created which could lead to an opportunity to become a Direct Endorsement underwriter - *i.e.:* a DE underwriter.

Product Training:
1. Fannie Mae and Freddie Mac home loan products
2. FHA home loan products
3. The one-time-close construction-to-perm loan
4. Down payment assistance programs
5. Loan underwriting processes
6. Account development/professional relationship cultivation
7. The FHA 203(k) home loan
8. Debt-to-income ratios
9. Loan-to-value (LTV)
10. Closing costs

Opportunities will exist for ____________ residents to be hired as __________ mortgage loan originators. The ____________ home office is located in ____________ . The development of home loan teams through our Proposal will enable __________ to expand the company's home loan origination platform and hiring processes in __________ .

By ascending to a management position, a ___________ resident could have an opportunity to open a branch office for the company. This will lead to further increases in hiring, staffing and training programs within _________. _________ will amend hiring and training processes as our Program is enacted, as per ___________ Labor Initiatives.

Vacant Houses, Developers and Developer Agreements

I had the opportunity to negotiate the acquisition of Land Bank properties in Kansas City, Missouri. Shortly thereafter, I read about how New York City could be moving towards utilizing a land bank.

People like to buy homes. People like it when home values increase. Homes in the center city Kansas City, MO, neighborhood that I focused on - the Blue Hills neighborhood - a few years after the fact, were selling at prices in the $110,000-range; an indication that home price appreciation was taking hold in center city Kansas City, Missouri, neighborhoods. Home price appreciation, that is, in the very same neighborhoods in which a notable portion of Land Bank properties were located. The acquisition cost of the Land Bank homes that I was involved with? *$2,000 per Land Bank home.*

"Every person who invests in well-selected real estate in a growing section of a prosperous community adopts the surest and safest method of becoming independent, for real estate is the basis of wealth." - Theodore Roosevelt

Replacing the electrical systems is oftentimes required of new owners when rehabbing a Land Bank home. These non-performing Kansas City homes in many cases have been abandoned, neglected and forgotten for years. Many homes are total rehabs, say, $45k per Land Bank home rehab, all-in, overall, on average. $45K in home rehab costs - *on average* - plus (for the homes I was involved in) the $2,000 acquisition cost. Looking at the fundamentals of the property acquisitions, that $47,000 - the $2,000 acquisition cost plus the $45,000 cost of the rehab - is significantly *less* than the $110,000 average market value of neighborhood homes. Price points of these homes equate to good fundamentals when assessing real estate development strategies which involve acquiring and rehabbing Land Bank properties.

"A funny thing happens in real estate. When it comes back, it comes back up like gangbusters." - Barbara Corcoran

Kansas City Land Bank home rehabs tend to be rather extensive projects to take on. Rehabbing a Land Bank home is, simply stated, not for the faint-of-heart. These are not quick and easy home rehabs. It would be inaccurate to represent them as such. One objective for Land Bank homes is to transition the homes to owner occupying buyers who bring the homes to "performing" status. Real estate practitioners who are considering taking on a project which involves rehabbing Land Bank homes might initially bring with them a fix-and-flip mentality. Yet a fix-and-flip approach would *not* be the correct perspective to have when acquiring and rehabbing Land Bank properties. An emphasis which is placed upon transitioning owner-occupying home buyers into rehabbed Land Bank homes through the use of low down payment affordable home loans is a sounder approach.

OK, so from Kansas City, let's travel 1,300 miles east to see how New Jersey's land bank processes work…

In New Jersey, municipalities can enter into land banking agreements with redevelopment entities. At which time, a municipality can designate redevelopment entities as land bank entities for a municipality. The aforementioned land banking agreement entered into between a municipality and a land bank entity would thus enable the redevelopment entity to lease and/or to convey properties which are owned by the municipality.

Within land banking agreements in New Jersey, responsibilities are specified for participating parties. Responsibilities applicable to how the land banking entity may acquire properties on behalf of the municipality and make improvements to properties once the properties have been acquired.

In New Jersey there is a program prerequisite to establish a community advisory board within six months of being designated as a land bank entity by a municipality.

OK, so what is a community advisory board anyway? And why is it a requirement to establish a community advisory board?

Land banks exist today within municipalities, and they really owe their existence to high numbers of vacant, distressed and non-performing properties which continue to create challenges for municipalities; challenges pertaining to how municipalities deal with these neighborhood liabilities. Because the private market really cannot solve this problem by itself. *"Mr. Market"* is not *"Mr. Fix It"* when it comes to the issue of, *What to do with non-performing properties owned by municipalities.* In a nutshell, land bank homes are non-performing properties that the private market has not absorbed and likely will not absorb, left to its own behaviors.

There are understandable reasons for why the private market has rejected these properties altogether, and may continue to reject these properties too. Among them, *1)* years of back taxes owed, *2)* clouded titles, *3)* rehab budgets which often exceed values of land bank homes after homes have been rehabbed, *4)* limited comps which can be used for appraisals, *5)* and this question, *Will owner-occupying home buyers be able to obtain a loan if they purchase a land bank home?*

How about the topic of small loan amounts? Oftentimes mortgage lenders just don't love small loan amounts. Then too, complexities associated with the FHA 203(k) loan. And so on, and so on, and so on... Challenges, and lots of them. Challenges, yet one objective for land banks is to transition these challenges - *i.e.:* these now-neighborhood liabilities - into "performing" neighborhood assets. While land bank properties come with very real challenges, high numbers of non-performing properties within a municipality create much larger challenges for the municipality, overall.

"Ninety percent of all millionaires become so through owning real estate." - Andrew Carnegie

Single-unit fix-and-flip home rehabs simply do not address the aforementioned collective neighborhood challenges for municipalities. Nor can a fix-and-flip approach address high numbers of vacant and abandoned properties strewn throughout the United States. A fix-and-flip business model is useful in a "onesies-twosies" business function for individual investors. But not for a city. The fix-

and-flip approach is not neighborhood-centric either. Hence, the interest and the motivation found in establishing land banking agreements with redevelopment entities. With land bank entities. *In New Jersey.*

Nationwide, just about 1.5 million homes sit vacant. At one time, New Jersey had nearly 400,000 vacant properties situated throughout the state. That 400,000 number was *before COVID-19.* One could assume that that number - 400,000 vacant homes in New Jersey - could very well go up. And it could go up by quite a bit. COVID-19 in all likelihood will prove to be a major contributor to challenges emanating from vacant New Jersey properties, and vacant properties throughout the United States as well. Yet, the inclination held by most in real estate with whom I have discussed this subject tends to be based upon a single-property acquisition-and-rehab business model. However, the single-property approach is rather ineffective when it comes to pursuing the establishment of a land bank real estate development program. So let's think about those New Jersey land banking agreements. Let's also think through objectives behind establishing those land banking agreements in the first place. *And let's think about New Jersey.*

A few years ago, the City of Newark had over six-thousand vacant properties. Marlboro, in Monmouth County, New Jersey? At one time Marlboro had over three-hundred vacant properties. Trenton? Nearly four-thousand vacant properties. Holmdel? Over one-hundred. Irvington? Nearly three-thousand vacant properties. Vernon? Over six-hundred. Jersey City? Over four-thousand. Toms River had over two-thousand vacant properties. Two-thousand vacant properties in Toms River - that's a lot of properties! Some of these municipalities are small-to-midsize cities. Some are suburbs. Some are larger deindustrialized cities. Some are municipalities with multi-million dollar homes. *It's a statewide problem.* These were vacant property totals from a few years ago, *before COVID-19.* Thousands of vacant properties in one state alone - *1.5 million vacant properties nationwide.*

In New Jersey, post-Pandemic, the State proceeded to add back a good portion of the jobs that had been lost due to the Pandemic. Those lost jobs made it more difficult for families to make their mortgage payments and pay their taxes. Taking into account high numbers of underutilized properties, pre-Pandemic, then taking into account properties that entered into default as a result of the Pandemic, New Jersey could benefit from real estate developers who choose to participate - along with municipalities - in land bank agreements and developer agreements. Pursuing real estate development projects could be aligned with objectives established by New Jersey municipalities in the transitioning of non-performing properties to "performing" status. This approach is a good framework under which to operate in New Jersey as a real estate developer.

In New Jersey, land bank entities adopt policies so as to ensure that community advisory boards are provided with pertinent property information and are kept up-to-date. This enables community advisory boards to provide input into decisions made by land bank entities. Community advisory boards serve as stakeholders. Communities - along with those who live in communities - are stakeholders.

Furthermore, New Jersey land bank entities can work with municipalities - and with community advisory boards - to establish online databases. Online databases provide the public with information about sale prices of land bank properties purchased by land bank entities.

In New Jersey, annual reports are to be furnished to municipalities by land bank entities. Within the annual reports, land bank entities would provide data pertinent to properties which are being held by the land bank entity, as well as what functions the land bank entity performed over the prior year.

When one logs onto the Detroit Land Bank Authority website, one might see, *Own it Now*, and, *$1,000,* as well as the hours, the minutes and the seconds remaining for one to acquire Detroit properties. This would be a one-by-one, single-property real estate acquisition function. Helpful, yes. Helpful for individual families in Detroit who have a nice opportunity to own their own home and to own their own home affordably, thanks to the Land Bank. Yet, arguably, real estate developers and large-scale redevelopment projects are what will prove to be most effective in terms of revitalization efforts in Detroit, based upon the high number of vacant lots and distressed properties in Detroit.

Much tends to be written about distressed properties in Detroit. Yet this challenge is one which is nationwide in scope. Small towns often encounter the same challenges larger cities such as Detroit encounter, albeit on a smaller scale.

A few years ago Brick Township in New Jersey had over one-thousand six-hundred vacant properties. A few years ago, Clifton, NJ, had over two-thousand vacant properties. A few years ago Elizabeth, NJ, had over one-thousand seven-hundred vacant properties. Vacant properties are a nationwide challenge. Or, looking at this another way, providing solutions to challenges resulting from non-performing properties municipalities own is a nationwide opportunity for real estate developers.

Taking into account the aforementioned high numbers of vacant properties owned by municipalities, in 2018, while the number of vacant houses dropped in Michigan - *dropped by 4%* - the number of vacant houses in Michigan's largest city - Detroit - *actually increased by nearly 30%.* At which time, just about one-quarter of Detroit's total housing stock was vacant. That's Detroit. In Cooks County, Illinois…home to Chicago? In 2018 there were about fifty-thousand vacant houses in Cooks County.. *Fifty-thousand.*

When choosing to invest in real estate, prospective buyers look to attain one or more of the following benefits: *a)* a low acquisition cost, *b)* little-to-no tenant stress (if a rental property), and *c)* steady appreciation: *a-b-c.* Yet one clear way to get to *a-b-c* would be a potential real estate path for buyers which is arguably all too often overlooked.

A real estate investor and/or an owner-occupying home buyer might like to know that *a-b-c* created America's first multi-millionaire, John Jacob Astor. Yet, arguably, too few real estate investors opt to pursue a real estate investment strategy comparable to that which America's first multimillionaire used to become America's first multi-millionaire - *a-b-c.*

While savvy real estate investors - as well as America's first multimillionaire - often focus their efforts on the acquisition of non-performing properties, owning real estate as an owner-occupant cannot be reasonably over-emphasized in terms of homeownership's applicability and overall importance to the financial well-being of American families. This is especially so when understanding that median housing equity makes up *over seventy-five percent* of overall net worth. *Investing in real estate and owning your own home as an owner-occupant works!*

"Real Estate cannot be lost or stolen, nor can it be carried away. Purchased with common sense, paid for in full, and managed with reasonable care, it is about the safest investment in the world." - Franklin D. Roosevelt

Vacant, distressed, abandoned and non-performing properties...

With a goal to stabilize neighborhoods while encouraging redevelopment in underserved communities, land banks assemble, manage, own and dispose of vacant land and abandoned properties. *Neighborhood-centric real estate development.*

According to a report by the Brookings Institute, an estimated 15% of land in major American cities is vacant. Vacant land and distressed non-performing properties do not produce adequate property tax revenue for cities, as property taxes function as a primary source for city revenue (or a lack thereof). With diminished property tax revenue coming into a city, the city could then be forced to consider making cuts to city services. In turn, impeding the availability of vital services families rely on.

Vacant, distressed, abandoned and non-performing properties are owned by municipalities...

Let's look at one city in particular, that city being St. Louis, Missouri. Over time, St. Louis took possession of an estimated 10,000 non-performing parcels of land. The 10,000 properties consisted of distressed residential houses, vacant lots and vacant buildings.

By conveying city-owned non-performing properties to developers, cities such as St. Louis can avoid serving as a de-facto property manager. Snow removal, mowing lawns and so on and so on... Burdensome property management responsibilities can be transferred by cities to qualified developers. Developers who acquire non-performing city-owned properties and who then proceed to repurpose properties as "performing" properties, adding properties back onto a city's tax roll.

Municipalities, cities, towns and land banks do not use multiple listing services to sell their properties. So let's look at how the City of St. Louis, Missouri, conveys city-owned properties.

St. Louis

The origin of the Land Reutilization Authority in St. Louis goes back to Title 1 of the Housing and Community Development Act of 1974. Funding for the LRA came from HUD and from the Community Development Administration.

In St. Louis, when submitting an offer to acquire a Land Reutilization Authority property, a prospective buyer submits their Offer To Purchase Form to the LRA. Their Offer To Purchase is accompanied by a $25.00 cashier's check, the buyer's two most recent pay stubs, two years W2's and tax returns, their most recent bank statement, their source of funding and a Planning Sheet too. The Planning Sheet is an overview for what the prospective buyer proposes to do - post-purchase - to improve the non-performing LRA property.

The conveyance of city-owned properties - and land banking for that matter - have been ever-evolving case studies, city-by-city, handled at the local level. Yet at the federal level, the first piece of federal legislation to address land banking was passed in 2008.

Resulting from the Financial Crisis of 2007 - 2008, Congress passed the Housing and Economic Recovery Act of 2008. The Housing and Economic Recovery Act appropriated $4 billion to address abandoned and foreclosed properties. The Housing And Economic Recovery Act of 2008 later became the Neighborhood Stabilization Program (NSP). In 2009, through the NSP, Congress appropriated an additional $2 billion to address vacant and abandoned properties.

The conveyance of city-owned properties…

A few years ago, St. Louis placed 522 LRA homes in their Dollar House Program. The 522 non-performing St. Louis properties entered into the Program had been owned by the LRA for at least five years and had been vacant for at least five years. Needless to say, the 522 Dollar House Program properties needed quite a bit of "TLC."

In St. Louis' Dollar Program a prospective owner-occupying home buyer was to first inspect the LRA home they intended to acquire, while also creating a rehab budget which was to be submitted when the buyer applied with the LRA. After a buyer's application had been submitted to the LRA, the application was reviewed by the LRA board. If the prospective LRA buyer was deemed to have met Program qualifications, with board approval, within one-hundred twenty days of purchasing the property, the new property owner was required to, *1)* stabilize the home, *2)* improve the facade of the home, and *3)* meet building codes.

The renovation of a St. Louis Dollar Program home was to be completed by the owner within eighteen months of acquisition. Furthermore, the buyer was required to rehab the home and live in the home for at least three years. LRA would hold a quitclaim deed to the property. The LRA's quit claim deed enabled the LRA to reclaim the property if the buyer failed to complete the rehab of the property according to requirements established through the property conveyance. Extensions in time to complete the home rehab were considered by the LRA if (or when) the rehab took longer than eighteen months.

Buying $1.00 distressed rundown homes in St. Louis, Missouri, to rehab? *Seriously?* Buying vacant land and run-down buildings in St. Louis, Missouri? *Seriously?* Buying rundown homes and vacant land anywhere? *Seriously?*

So a little perspective. The underdeveloped, non-performing, overlooked and sometimes sneered-upon vacant land that John Jacob Astor long ago purchased on his way to becoming America's first multimillionaire? What was that land? Where was that land? What overlooked part of America was Mr. Astor interested in? Where was that barren and forgotten land located? Well, that under-developed, overlooked, vacant land we are speaking of is what we know today to be…*Manhattan.*

A land bank is OK for certain cities but New York City is different. Oh really?

In one New York Times op-ed piece, New York City Council Member Brad Lander articulated how a land bank could put properties to productive use in a manner which would serve local communities in neighborhoods in which non-performing properties are located. The New York Times op-ed piece was titled, *How To Avoid a Post-Recession Feeding Frenzy by Private Developers.*

"Wall Street, Broadway and Soho boomed, but artists and average workers couldn't afford to live here. Small-business owners started new ventures but were priced out of affordable commercial space. Immigrant families worked hard but struggled mightily to pay skyrocketing rents." - Brad Lander, September 2, 2020, The New York Times

Excellent points! In New York State, municipalities are able to create land banks, as too then would be New York City.

The purpose of land banks in New York State is to provide requisite resources, direction, vision, personnel and funding to enable municipalities to deal with non-performing properties. Land banks are established to improve neighborhoods while at the same time reducing development challenges.

Non-performing properties in New York State tax districts are not on tax rolls of New York municipalities. Not being on tax rolls…non-performing properties do not generate property tax revenue for New York State tax districts. The lack thereof culminates in holes in annual budgets for New York State tax districts. *i.e.:* Budget gaps.

Land banks acquire vacant and abandoned properties. Land banks do a great job by transitioning non-performing properties to developers. Developers who have the ability to rehab, to renovate and to improve land bank properties they acquire. Once improved, land bank properties can then be sold, thus returning once non-performing properties to neighborhoods as "performing" properties. As such, repurposed neighborhood properties create additional property tax revenue for New York State tax districts. Simply stated, non-performing properties do not. Section 1608 of Assembly Bill A373A spoke to a land bank's acquisition of properties in New York State. Section 1609 of A373A spoke to a land bank's disposition of properties in New York State.

Former New York Governor Andrew Cuomo signed New York State's Land Bank Law into effect on July 29, 2011. In doing so, New York State municipalities gained an ability by way of the Albany legislature to establish land banks in the State of New York. In New York, land banks operate under the New York State Urban Development Corporation.

According to an article published in *The Patch - High-Income New Yorkers to City: We're Thinking Of Leaving You* - one interesting survey indicated that over 40% of survey respondents making over $100,000 per year have considered leaving New York City. Furthermore, according to *The Patch*, 37% of survey respondents indicated that it was "likely" that they would not be residing in New York City in two years. Housing affordability, or a lack thereof, affects more than those who live in neighborhoods with high concentrations of non-performing properties.

In New York State, municipalities that are able to establish land banks include, *a)* cities, *b)* villages, *c)* towns, and *d)* counties. To establish a land bank, a New York municipality would first establish an entity to function as what is known as a foreclosing governmental unit. The foreclosing governmental unit operates within guidelines established through local laws, local ordinances and local resolutions. These laws, ordinances and resolutions specify parameters by which cities, villages, towns and counties - *i.e.*: municipalities - are able to establish processes which enable the municipality to function as the foreclosing governmental entity. *I.e.:* as the land bank. Oversight and governance for New York State land banks is the responsibility of land bank boards of directors. As per Assembly Bill A373A, parameters for land bank boards of directors fall within Section 1605, of A373A.

Land Bank board membership can total between five and fifteen members. The number of land bank board members will be an odd number; a number between five and fifteen.

In 1980, New York City spending, adjusted for inflation - including only local dollars - was $29 billion. The $29 billion did not take into account federal or state aid. In 2019 New York City spending totaled $69 billion. The City's Financial Control Board evaluates budgets.

In 1975, some lenders cut off New York City from borrowing. New York City at one time had been on the cusp of bankruptcy. Detroit filed for bankruptcy in July of 2013. New York City was once almost there itself. As New Yorkers leave New York City and as New York City businesses close, additional stresses are placed upon the City. *A strain on any city's budget.*

No one is saying that New York City will one day become Detroit. That will not occur. This being said, Councilman Brad Lander's New York Times op-ed piece spoke to challenges which could develop as byproducts of a recession. As byproducts of accompanying budget constraints, coupled to budget shortfalls. Very insightful perspective provided by Councilman Lander.

Councilman Brad Lander's New York Times op-ed piece also cited effective ways to manage city processes coming out of a recession, processes that can fall within operations of a well-run land bank. Formed in a time of budgetary constraints. Formed to address real estate concerns which land banks are very well-suited to address. Real estate solutions which can be brought to New York City through the establishment of a land bank.

At the height of the COVID-19 Pandemic, in excess of 5,000 New York City businesses closed over one six-month period. During this same six-month period, the number of residential real estate listings in New York City increased by upwards of 80%, evidencing an inclination for New Yorkers to sell their residences and cash out with the help of elevated real estate values. Then too (in many cases) leave New York City. Then there is that aforementioned survey conducted by *The Patch.* The survey, which spoke to how a substantive number of New Yorkers have considered leaving New York City altogether. Housing affordability continues to be a challenge in New York City.

There is certainly no predicted financial demise for New York City. However, one can certainly argue - citing housing affordability (or a lack thereof) - that Governor Cuomo acted very wisely in July of 2011 when he signed the Land Bank Law into effect. With the Land Bank Law in place in New York, Councilman Lander is also correct in citing benefits which could be realized in New York City neighborhoods through the establishment of a New York City land bank.

New York City Councilman Brad Lander was born in the great State of Missouri. In 2012, the Missouri State Legislature authorized establishment of land banks by ordinance or resolution. St. Louis has the oldest land bank in the United States. In 1971, the Land Reutilization Authority was established in St. Louis.

Councilman Brad Lander is a City Council Member representing New York City's 39th District. Councilman Brad Lander's District includes Boerum Hill, Brooklyn Heights, Park Slope, Flatbush and Borough Park - *five prime development areas*. These are neighborhoods which have been and which will continue to be prioritized by real estate developers.

Question: What might have been among one of the topics the City Council considered in January of 2018 in the Committee on Housing and Buildings in New York City?

Answer: A Local Law to amend the administrative code of New York City in relation to creating a land bank. A Local Law to establish a land bank for New York City. A Local Law co-sponsored by Councilman Brad Lander and Councilman Justin L. Brannon. Councilman. Justin L. Brannon represented New York City's 43rd District.

Kansas City, Missouri, established their land bank in 2012. By 2021, in my home state of Kansas, twenty-three Kansas cities along with one Kansas county passed local ordinances to allow for the establishment of land banks. Here's to hoping that the wise insight demonstrated by then-Governor Cuomo in signing New York's Land Bank Law, coupled to a connection Councilman Lander has to the State which has the oldest land bank in the country - Missouri - prove to be enough to get New York City to establish their own land bank.

Redevelopment: Looking at an approach used in Red Bank...

In Red Bank, New Jersey, The Galleria Red Bank - today, a quaint collection of offices, restaurants and boutiques located in the heart of what some refer to as "New Jersey's Greenwich Village" - was built over a ten-year period early in the Twentieth Century.

Between the years of 1907 and 1917, The Galleria - originally known as the Eisner Building - was constructed with an endgame in mind which is not too similar at all to what The Galleria is known to be today. The Galleria of today is a redeveloped Red Bank centerpiece located right where Bridge Avenue meets West Front Street. No, that original early Twentieth Century endgame for The Galleria did not involve chic restaurants. No, that original early Twentieth Century endgame for The Galleria did not involve enticingly charming retail outlets. Rather, that original early-Twentieth Century endgame was predicated on an idea of The Galleria functioning *as a textile factory.*

During both World Wars, The Galleria was a township stalwart which did not espouse a trendy retail "DNA." Rather, The Galleria of long-ago-Red Bank once possessed an industrial "DNA," serving as a vital supply chain hub for World War I and World War II American military equipment - flight suits, military uniforms and gas masks, each representing wartime supplies which once made up a consortium of items produced for American soldiers in Red Bank at The Galleria, early in the Twentieth Century.

In New Jersey, a Redevelopment Area is correlated to the topic of, *What to do with blight?* More specifically, Redevelopment Areas relate to blighted areas. Areas where, once that blight has been redeveloped, revitalization of the community as a whole will likely take place.

In a designated Redevelopment Area, a municipality's goals could be focused upon transitioning non-performing residential, commercial and industrial properties to vibrant community assets. The pursuit of which takes on a community-centric theme: *renovations, repurposing properties and reconstruction.* Each of these are goals pursuant to redeveloping non-performing properties in designated Redevelopment Areas.

Steps taken by a municipality in their progression towards revitalization in Redevelopment Areas. Progression, that is, coupled to a redevelopment plan emanating from city hall. And this often starts off with city council passing a resolution. Following a resolution, a planning board then might construct a Redevelopment map. With a Redevelopment map formulated, and upon notification to the public of a scheduled hearing, the planning board could then potentially adopt a Redevelopment resolution. An adopted Redevelopment resolution could recommend the establishment of a Redevelopment Area within a municipality. There is quite a bit more technical minutiae to this process, needless to say. Yet, in summarily-simplified terms, this is how we can thus arrive at the designation of a Redevelopment Area within a municipality.

On July 23, 2019, resulting from a unanimous vote undertaken by Red Bank Commissioners, the Red Bank Redevelopment Agency was created. In Red Bank, the Redevelopment Agency prioritized redevelopment efforts which benefit the Red Bank community, positively impacting the lives of those who reside in Red Bank. It was constructed to be a community-centric redevelopment and revitalization "tool."

Today, there are eight retail outlets in the once-a-textile-hub Galleria. Today, there are four restaurants located in the once-a-textile-hub Galleria. Buffalo wings, pizza, Thai food and Mexican food. Each is now available to enjoy at The Galleria, thanks to planned redevelopment efforts undertaken in Red Bank.

Tracing back thirty years ago to the origin of the transformation of what is now a collection of fine amenities at The Galleria, in the early 1990's circumstances at The Galleria were quite different. In the early 1990's, The Galleria had not yet been redeveloped.

Utilizing "tools" made available to New Jersey municipalities, along with redevelopment "road maps" established in Trenton, Red Bank used resources available through redevelopment to designate an entity in the early 1990's to manage the restoration of The Galleria. This redevelopment took place within a special improvement district.

A special improvement district is a Business Improvement District. It's an area within a municipality where businesses pay an additional tax which goes towards funding redevelopment projects undertaken in the designated district. In Red Bank, as per redevelopment, today's "fruits of labor" that one finds at The Galleria trace their origin back to Red Bank's use of redevelopment tools which are made available to municipalities such as Red Bank through Trenton.

There are five offices in the once-a-textile-hub Galleria. That early-Twentieth

Century factory at The Galleria, long ago producing American military uniforms, once "majored" in textiles. Today, that old factory now "majors" in the provision of office space, restaurants and retail. *Each the result of redevelopment.*

Pursuant to redevelopment, New Jersey municipalities are required to reexamine their master plans at least once every ten years. Red Bank attempted to be proactive in this manner through their establishment of the Red Bank Redevelopment Agency.

Two noted objectives established by the Red Bank Redevelopment Agency were, *1)* to complete an inventory of Borough-owned properties, to assess zoning status and to perform a highest-and-best-use analysis, and *2)* to support preservation of single family, owner-occupied homes. Priorities in Red Bank included transitioning non-performing properties now owned by the municipality to be repurposed. Thus increasing the availability of single-family homes in Red Bank.

So let's do a quick, *OK, this is how they do it here, and this is how they do it there...*

In Kansas City, a good friend of mine previously served as the Executive Director for the Land Bank of Kansas City of Kansas City, Missouri. While Kansas City, Missouri, utilized their Land Bank to transition non-performing properties in KC to developers and to rehabbers, Red Bank, New Jersey, does not at the present time utilize a comparable land bank model to transition properties owned by Red Bank to developers. Land banks are rather new in the State of New Jersey. Governor Murphy signed the New Jersey Lank Bank Law into effect on July 11, 2019. By contrast, in Kansas City, the Kansas City Land Bank went into effect seven years prior to the signing of the New Jersey Land Bank Law - in 2012.

For New Jersey municipalities which do not have a land bank, procedures to transition properties owned by municipalities to developers, while remaining aligned with municipality redevelopment plans, can be effectuated through the issuance of a Request For Proposals (RFP) or a Request For Qualifications (RFQ) .

What is interesting (with some added complexity) about township redevelopment procedures in New Jersey as compared to Kansas City and the Kansas City Land Bank, is that in New Jersey, once a planning board designates a Redevelopment

Area within a municipality, that municipality is required to forward their local resolution to the New Jersey Department of Community Affairs (DCA). At which time, if the designated Redevelopment Area is not located in an area where development/redevelopment is sought after pursuant to objectives set forth in Trenton, the Redevelopment Area designation would then be predicated upon the issuance of a final approval by the DCA.

Beginning each year on Mother's Day, then continuing on through November, the Farmers Market in Red Bank at The Galleria owes its weekly collection of vegetables to local farmers. Farmers' locally-grown produce is enjoyed by swaths of market-goers every Sunday in-season at The Galleria in Red Bank. A community benefit made possible by Red Bank redevelopment efforts.

The 100,000 square foot Galleria, today a beautifully rustic multi-purpose building, is situated on nearly-three acres of redeveloped land in the heart of Red Bank. Today, The Galleria serves as a visible representation of what redevelopment really looks like when community-centric revitalization efforts are enacted.

"Decisions of the agency will be made transparently and with input from the community..." - a stated priority established by The Redevelopment Agency of the Borough of Red Bank..

With an eye on what is in store in Red Bank, it's a good idea for those who live, who work, and who love Red Bank to participate in redevelopment discussions in a manner which is aligned with redevelopment efforts in Red Bank, *"...with input from the community."*

Redevelopment: One concept is a transit village

In March 2014, Plainfield, NJ, became the 6th transit village - *or, transit village hub* - in Union County, NJ, and the 28th transit village in the State of New Jersey. Pleasantville was the State's first transit village, designated as such in 1999.

If one knows New Jersey, the State has a few obvious transit villages. Among them? Montclair, Morristown and Hoboken. If you have ever visited Montclair, Morristown or Hoboken, one might correctly surmise that a transit village hub is a pedestrian-friendly neighborhood. It's a quick commute into New York City. It's a neighborhood where people can live, shop, work and play without needing to own or lease a car. In New Jersey, a transit village designation comes through the Department of Transportation and New Jersey Transit. Hence, evidencing the correlation to, *"...without needing to own or lease a car.*

Smart planning, vision and collaboration…

The City of Plainfield identified real estate development located near a train station as a priority. So in 2010, the City began to work with the New Jersey Institute of Technology to organize a report based upon transit-oriented development projects. Then, beginning in 2011, Plainfield started to work with the Transit Village Task Force with an eye on earning the transit village designation. That designation occurred three years later, in 2014. The Transit Village Task Force is a group of ten New Jersey State agencies.

Fast forward to 2018. In 2018 in Plainfield we witnessed, *a)* the announcement of a half-billion dollar redevelopment plan, *b)* the city's return to the state's business tax-friendly Urban Enterprise Zone, *c)* plans for a $1.3 million transformation of North Avenue, and *d)* plans for several downtown construction projects. Plans which would ideally correlate to an additional one-thousand residential units, and to more than forty-thousand square feet of retail space.

Digressing back to, *...without needing to own or lease a car,* North Avenue in Plainfield has been slated to transition into a bustling entertainment center. *I.e.:* a transit village with that easy pedestrian walk to the City's train station.

New Home Construction: the S.O.V. (Schedule of Values)

Applicable to new home construction, the success of any new home build is reliant upon provision of well-communicated - and clear - expectations to key project stakeholders, while simultaneously maintaining overall project transparency. As such, it is important to list, to organize, to put into sequence and to understand each project expenditure. Labor, materials and supplies, each listed as a total dollar amount, and as an individual percentage of the project.

Receipts and invoices for labor and supplies, specific to work performed by contractors and subcontractors within each phase of construction, should be reviewed on an ongoing basis in accordance with pre-project timelines and budgets. Supplies and materials used during draw periods of the build should be itemized. Itemization enables comprehensive project supervision by stakeholders to take place as the project progresses. One example which is illustrative of how proper categorization of receipts, invoices and labor costs can function as a requirement in order for the success of the project to take place can be observed in looking at how construction loans are used to finance new home builds.

With new home construction, when the home build is financed with a construction loan, a detailed itemization for work performed - coupled to building supplies - is provided to the lender by way of a draw request. Having itemized costs properly organized prior to submitting a draw request to the lender is an important step to take. Doing so accurately can ensure that a timely release of funds by the lender to the builder, as per the builder's submitted draw request, takes place.

Lenders providing financing for new home construction carefully review each draw request. With a construction loan, specific itemization of expenditures, of tasks performed and of labor allocated to project progression within an established draw period should be communicated to the lender in a clear and concise manner. In this example - financing the new home build with a construction loan - the lender's progress reviews could be used as an example for how project oversight can be adhered to, notwithstanding review process(es) initiated by project stakeholders. *I.e.:* the property owner, contractors, subcontractors, the architect, investors and so on…

When a construction loan draw request has been submitted to a lender, the lender's internal loan review process begins. Documents are analyzed by the lender. Inspections are ordered by the lender. Lender inspections ensure that scheduled work is completed within the draw period. Done so in accordance with plan projections. This is all verified by the lender prior to the release of funds in response to the draw request.

It goes without saying that neither the property owner nor the contractor would be the lender. Yet home build details studied by the lender in loan review process(es) can be understood, then applied to the project's supervision by the property owner and/or by the contractor. So as to ensure the success of the project.

This brings us to the S.O.V.: Schedule of Values

As construction commences, then moves forward, the success of the project will rely upon each stakeholder being able to correlate work performed in a given draw period to money spent and to timelines established. It is important for the lender to verify that work has been completed within the draw period to funds requested to be released in accordance with a draw request.

When building a new home, tasks which need to be completed in order for the successful completion of the home build to occur - tasks completed by contractors and subcontractors during draw periods - can be memorialized in the project's schedule of values. Progressing in chronological order, the schedule of values assigns a payment value and a percentage to each itemization included in the schedule. The schedule of values lists the cost of work which is to be completed, while also communicating to stakeholders what that cost represents as a total project percentage. This takes place with the S.O.V. in each draw period.

The property owner, contractors, subcontractors, investors, the lender, project stakeholders, the architect as well as project managers are able to stay updated on progress of the home build through the schedule of values. The schedule of values relates to billable work performed and to tasks completed during each draw period. As each phase of the home build has been completed - *i.e.:* as one draw period progresses to the next draw period - the project's schedule of values is updated. The updating of the S.O.V. in subsequent draw periods is directly relatable to forthcoming draw requests. For each new draw request, line items in the schedule of values, as per project progression in each draw period, are revised.

When discussing new home construction, it goes without saying that in-sequence completion of stages of the build by contractors and subcontractors - as will be outlined in the schedule of values - is tantamount in terms of importance, prior to subsequent build project tasks being undertaken (and financed). For example, one cannot start on the framing of a new home without a foundation. A foundation for the home is a set project cost, as is the framing. Each would be itemized in the S.O.V. as a total dollar amount of the project and as a percentage of the project too. *Within the S.O.V.*

The laying of the foundation as well as framing are each scheduled within the scope of the project. Timelines for each would be established prior to the breaking of ground. The schedule of values serves as a sort of "itemized directional." A map, or directions, so-to-speak for tasks completed and for money which is being spent to finance the completion of those individual tasks within each draw period. When building a new home, the schedule of values is a good tool to use so as to ensure that each integrated-yet-separate phase of the project stays on track, with measured accountability.

Let's look at what a schedule of values might look like…

With a new home build, say the plans and specs run at a cost of $3,000. So, within the schedule of values, that $3,000 cost for plans and specs would be a set dollar amount allotted as a specific component within the overall project - *"plans and specs."* Within the S.O.V. that same $3,000 for plans and specs would also be categorized as a percentage of the project. If project costs are $125,000 in total, while plans and specs run at a cost of $3,000, then within the S.O.V., plans and specs would be categorized as 2.4% of the overall project. Itemized as a dollar amount - $3,000 - and as a project percentage - 2.4% - within the S.O.V.

We looked at how plans and specs could be included in the S.O.V. Let's now look at a second example. That second example? Rough framing.

If rough framing for the project runs at a total cost $30,000, then rough framing will be categorized within the S.O.V. as 20% of overall project costs. Rough framing within the S.O.V. will be categorized as a dollar amount - $30,000 - and as a project percentage - 20%.

Why use a Schedule of Values for a new home build?

The S.O.V. is a great management tool and is very effective for regular payment applications when payment schedules are chosen in lieu of larger less-frequent lump sum payments. Furthermore, utilizing the S.O.V. provides stakeholders with flexibility if and when changes need to be made to schedules. Or to costs within the project.

Whereas notifying each stakeholder of build plan changes, one-by-one, would be what could occur if a S.O.V. is not utilized, project changes can be encapsulated within the S.O.V., then shared with each project stakeholder through the S.O.V. This is a cleaner way to ensure that clear and concise communication takes place among stakeholders if and when any changes need to be made to project plans, materials and/or costs.

New Home Construction: Land Grading

Your goal is to build a new home. New home construction. For your new home build, the property surface - *i.e.:* the land on which your new home will be built - is literally and figuratively, *the foundation to it all.*

With single-family new home construction, before your home builder breaks ground on the project, as the property owner, you will want to ensure that steps have been taken to clear and to level your buildable residential lot. A foundation for your new home soon will be poured. Any holes found in the property's surface should be filled in. This ensures that the foundation for your new home will be poured on a land surface which has optimal conditions applicable to new home construction.

The foundation will soon be in, so it's a good idea to use wooden stakes to mark where exactly the foundation will ultimately be poured. If your property turns out to have an uneven surface - *i.e.:* hills, recesses, dips, mounds, holes... - the next step is grading.

So while a flat, level lot is, early on in the process of planning your new home build, what your goal would be, as you approach the pouring of your foundation, an entirely flat level lot with no slope whatsoever throughout the entire property extending beyond your home's footprint is *not* a property surface condition to sustain. Which brings us to grading.

Grading is the structuring of the surface of the land area applicable to your new home build. To summarize, the property's grading is its slope. As per grading, it is important to ensure there will be proper slope added to the graded property surface. The ideal slope for your new home build is for the land on the outer perimeter of the home's foundation to descend away from your newly-built home. This decline - applicable to grading - is important because grading ultimately determines where rainwater, as well as where runoff water from the roof, will flow.

With a positive grade, land slopes away from your new home. Therefore, positive grade is the desired outcome for your new home build. Inasmuch as with positive grade, rainwater, as well as roof run-off, will be directed away from the foundation of your new home. This is ideal. Positive grade is also referred to as good soil grade.

In contrast to positive grade, negative grade slopes the property surface towards the foundation of your home. This slope would not be your desired outcome. Negative grade is also known as poor soil grade. Positive grade reduces the risk of erosion, thereby mitigating future foundation damage. With negative grade, erosion, and in turn, potential foundation damage, is more likely possible.

For every one foot that you move away from your new home build's footprint, you will want the ground surface for your property to drop one inch. This application - one foot/drop one inch - should be established for your home build footprint's perimeter, extending up to ten feet around the perimeter of the footprint.

In terms of "real estate speak," being a real estate broker myself, I often read property descriptions for marketed homes whereby the property description is written as having a *level lot.* In terms of your new home build, level is not the property surface condition you are looking for. Level, thereby, is not optimal.

We touched on the topic of positive grade. And in this section we also touched on the topic of negative grade. Positive grade, and negative grade. So we should also discuss level grade.

Level grade is a condition whereby the ground surface is, well, level. *I.e.:* flat. When building your new home, level grade is a property surface condition which needs to be corrected, not maintained. This correction can be accomplished through grading. For your new home build, you will want positive grade.

Level grade should be transitioned to positive grade so as to ensure there will be proper drainage around the foundation of your new home. This occurs when a property surface is sloped at the optimal decline. *I.e.:* positive grade. Thus with positive grade, rainwater, as well as roof run-off, flows away from the foundation of your new home. The then-trajectory of rainwater running away from your foundation reduces future risk of foundation damage.

What does grading cost? The typical cost for grading can run between $5.00 to $10.00 per square foot of the property.

New Home Construction: trusses have the advantage

A majority of home builders address the provision of adequate roof support for new home builds by using trusses. Trusses are engineered, prefabricated, triangular, wood support structures. Trusses are used by home builders more and more today, as opposed to a builder's reliance on 2-by-8's or 2-by-10's. 2-by-8's and 2-by-10's being roof support ingredients of fast-disappearing labor-intensive stick-built framing. By contrast, trusses are built with 2-by-4's as opposed to 2-by-8's or 2-by-10's which are used in stick-built framing. This is a cost-saving measure for home builders (and for home buyers too).

Furthermore, utilization of trusses by home builders can reduce a need to have some interior walls serve as load-bearing walls. This is a nice advantage for home buyers because there will then be more options available pertaining to where walls can be erected within the home according to a build plan. Since interior walls in the home will not then function as load-bearing - a benefit gained by building with trusses - interior walls can be taken down at a later date by the homeowner, if they so choose to redesign the interior of their home. The key point is, trusses do not need to rest on load-bearing walls. This leads to more interior design options for home buyers as their new home is being designed, coupled to the availability of more home updating options at a later date. Because trusses do not rest on load-bearing walls.

Nearly 80% of new homes built today are built with trusses. Trusses are factory-built, then shipped to construction sites. When building new homes without using trusses, roof support calculations will be based on assessments provided by home builders. This tends to leave much more to chance in relation to roof support. Rather, trusses are designed by engineers with design parameters formulated, with building codes in mind.

In terms of roof design, trusses facilitate lots of nice options for home buyers who may opt for a custom roof. Cathedral ceilings or cross gables? Either would be possible when crafting details for your home design by using trusses.

Open floor plans are very popular today. When opting for an open floor plan, your home builder will likely opt for scissor trusses. With scissor trusses, as the home buyer, you can then select high-sloped ceilings. A very nice feature, when paired with your open floor plan.

www.ingramcontent.com/pod-product-compliance
Lightning Source LLC
Chambersburg PA
CBHW071324130726
47996CB00002B/609